There's a Small Hotel

Published by Methuen 2000

1 3 5 7 9 10 8 6 4 2

First published in Great Britain in 2000 by
Methuen Publishing Limited
215 Vauxhall Bridge Road
London SW1V 1EJ

Methuen Publishing Limited Reg. No. 3543167

A CIP catalogue record for this book
is available from the British Library

ISBN 0 413 74370 5

Typeset by SX Composing DTP, Rayleigh, Essex
Printed and bound in Great Britain by
Creative Print & Design (Wales), Ebbw Vale

There's a Small Hotel

Nicky Hayward

Methuen

In memory of Lionel Albert Bailey, my dad.

Contents

Acknowledgements

Following a trip to Italy to watch an old school friend, Anthony Minghella, directing *The Talented Mr Ripley*, I returned with a literary agent and a commission to write a book. To this day I am not quite sure how it happened, but thank Anthony not only for his friendship, but also encouraging me to write; Michael Earley, David Salmo and all at Methuen for taking on a complete novice; Charlotte Hofton for guiding me through the whole process and casting an eye over all I did; Judy Daish and Eleo Carson, precious friends, who generously made time in their hectic professional lives to scoop me up and keep me going.

Artists, photographers, friends and business consultants who freely donated their time and professional skills: Julia and Ian Lamaison, Brian Palmer, John Burleigh, Denis O'Regan, Ben Wood, Sally Bulloch, Richard Peat, Patricia Yates, Pam Donald, Jessica Dobbs, Victor Ceserani, Lou Dorley Brown, Martin Begin-Jones.

Caroline Ali, who runs our home so I can help run our business.

My mum, the smartest business woman I know, and Uncle Jim who taught me to try to make it perfect.

Nick, my lovely supportive husband, close friend and confidant, who believes in me even when I don't believe in myself, and our three gorgeous children Ben, Pip and Jules.

Most of all to all employees past and present, all suppliers and everyone who has ever stayed or eaten at the Seaview Hotel and helped make our business the success it is today.

PREFACE

September
Entering a Small Hotel

Entering a good hotel or restaurant for the first time can, and should, be a dramatic moment. Standing on the threshold, you drift between insecurity and keen anticipation until you are officially greeted, welcomed and shown to your table or room. It's this initial greeting that Italian restaurateurs and *patrons* are so expert at: sweeping you up, as they do, like royalty or a long-lost relative and reassuringly guiding you through to a comfortable spot, even if it's to the smallest table or room. The special attention and care you are shown from the first moment will ensure your return again and again. First impressions *do* count. They certainly count in the kind of business my husband Nick and I run on the Isle of Wight.

This is the story of a year in the life of the Seaview Hotel and Restaurant, nestled in the north-east corner of the Island. We've been running our small hotel for nearly twenty years and business has never been better or busier. I am going to start this record of the year – my ship's log, if you like – on an overcast September morning, in the month when Nick and I originally took over this struggling hotel two decades ago. The frantic August Bank Holiday is over but this year, 1998, September will prove to be far from tranquil. For we are about to be assessed. Martin Bregin-Jones, a quality expert from BT, leads the team who, over three days and nights, search through our records for documentary evidence to support our original submission to the British Quality Foundation. They conduct extensive interviews not only with Nick and me, but with virtually our entire workforce. Assessing how we measure up against the Business Excellence Model. As I was embarrassingly to say on BBC local radio, 'it was just like having someone look through your knicker draw'.

We first came across the model in 1996. A simplified version was used to judge our winning entry in a local excellence competition conducted through the Island's chamber of commerce. In 1997 we went on to the regional awards run by Meridian Television in conjunction with the British Quality Foundation. Founded in 1992 following a government review, the BQF has as its principle 'to promote and advance the use of Business Excellence and Total Quality techniques in the UK'. Exactly what this has to do with the running of a small, sixteen-bedroomed hotel on the Isle of Wight did not seem immediately obvious to us.

Nick and I constantly wanted to raise standards in our small business. But working so closely together over many years, and coping not only with a commercial partnership but also with marriage and parenthood, meant it was sometimes hard to see the wood for the trees. Entering for an independent business award forced us to take a different and more objective view of our operation. It also enabled us to be analysed and judged by others with far greater commercial expertise than our own. It was free expert consultancy.

So following our submission to the regional competition in 1997, we found ourselves, along with three other finalists, in a Meridian Television studio with Carol Vorderman. After a formal dinner, just like the Oscars ceremony, Nick and I, surrounded by eight of our loyal employees, nervously awaited the result. The other two finalists were Vickers and a multimillion-pound housing association from Kent. It was billed for the viewers as a David and Goliath fight and we, the small hotel from the Isle of Wight, won.

Initially we were completely baffled by the business language. It took me weeks to appreciate that *human resources* and *strategy* meant *people* and *plans*. So when Meridian suggested we should now enter for the national UK Quality Award, we really felt the business terminology alone was beyond us. But John Burleigh, one of the original Meridian team who assessed the hotel, and who has since become our independent business consultant, kindly translated for us all the terms used in the Business Excellence model. Once we understood what it all meant we discovered it was a simple and effective way of looking at all aspects of our business and working towards continuous improvement. Divided into two parts, the model consists of Enablers and Results. Under Enablers were the

headings Leadership, People Management, Policy
& Strategy, Resources & Processes.

Now John explained that 'leadership' was Nick
and I; that was all right – we knew exactly what we
did. Then there was the way we delegated to our
employees and how they lead their teams: that was
'people management'. Once we had grasped that a
'strategy' was a plan, this was no problem – we
always had plenty of those. One difficulty was
'resources' and 'processes'. After a lesson from
John, we understood that even a raw carrot or
potato was an incoming resource. We also learnt
exactly what a process meant: The Model is all
about improvement; we hadn't realised that when
we invested in a new steam convection oven which
reduced the preparation time of our poached
meringues from two hours to a matter of minutes,
this was a vastly improved *process*.

The other section of the model, called Results, is
divided into People Satisfaction, Customer Satisfaction, Impact on Society, and Business Results.
Well, we soon appreciated that people satisfaction
was how happy our employees were, customer
satisfaction was obvious, and impact on society was
about the effect we had on our local community
and environment – all things very close to our
hearts. Finally, there were our figures and results, of
which we had accumulated plenty of details over
the years, and all of which were moving steadily up.

To enter for the national award we had to
prepare a thirty-page document giving in-depth
details and statistics about the hotel. John Burleigh

continued to guide us through the whole process of preparing and submitting the document. In June, 1998 when we heard we had qualified for a site visit and in-depth assessment, we knew we had a place in the finals. The awards were to be announced at a ceremony in London, in October. We discovered that the other UK finalists were DHL International, Vista Optics, Post Office Counters, BT Payphone, Nortel Northern Ireland, NatWest Insurance and a branch of the Inland Revenue. Now we really did feel completely out of our league.

CHAPTER 1

October
Recipe for Success

On the evening of Thursday 29th October 1998 Nick and I stand outside the Grosvenor House Hotel in London's West End, desperately peering into each arriving taxi. Hundreds of formally dressed men and glittering women were arriving for the gala dinner to celebrate the UK Quality Awards for Business Excellence. We, however, are searching for our three offspring and my mother, all of whom we have lost on our way to this grand hotel. Along with the seven other finalists, big businesses every one, we should be at the VIP drinks party to meet the financial media and the minister, Barbara Roche, from the Department of Trade and Industry. Instead Nick, looking distinguished in his dinner jacket and I, trying to look businesslike in a simply cut, black Nicole Farhi suit, are freezing outside the front doors of the hotel. Guests at the feast but not quite inside. Still no sign of the family.

This event, with all its business hype, is a far cry from the front door of our small hotel in Seaview, though not so far from that fast-paced London life we left twenty years earlier before we bought our 'dream hotel'. I feel completely daunted.

It was during the late 1970s that Nick and I, in our mid twenties, made the decision to give up our jobs and leave London to sail off into the unknown and chart a very different course. I was happy in the City of London with the highly respected independent wine merchants and restauranteurs Corney & Barrow. But after the birth of our son, Ben, I found myself in the trap of every young working mother – how to mix domestic bliss with a professional career? Nick, now a young deputy general manager at the Athenaeum Hotel on Piccadilly, would have to wait before he could become a top West End general manager, and at the time there were few de luxe London hotels he wanted to run. My reckless desire to plunge ahead into the unknown overrode Nick's natural caution and need to stick with the status quo. So, after a year of weighing up the options, we packed our bags and mortgaged ourselves to the hilt to take on a small rundown hotel on the Isle of Wight. It was going to be a real voyage of discovery.

I was convinced Nick had the natural flare and charm to host his own hotel, and, with him out front, immaculately presented and attentive to every guest's needs, I could apply my business skills and an extensive knowledge of wine, food and design to back him.

Our search for the dream location took us to Scotland, Yorkshire, Rutland and Norfolk before we decided to return to the village of Seaview. It was a real homecoming. Nick's family had come down to the Island for generations, and had family pictures of his grandmother on the old suspension pier at Seaview in 1890, while I had grown up only three miles down the road.

That first September night back in 1980, I lay in bed with our baby Ben, pregnant with our second child Pip, wondering what I had got us into. I thought of Nick downstairs alone, having left his staff of two hundred back at the Athenaeum, now on his hands and knees trying to sort out a plumbing problem in the gents' lavatory.

Finally, we realise that my mother and the young Haywards must have come in by another entrance. Reunited, we take our seats in the Great Room at the Grosvenor, the venue for huge charity balls and most large televised ceremonies in London including the Bafta and Sony awards. At the next table sit a team of loyal supporters and friends who have travelled up from the Island to be with us as spectators and to cheer us on. Amongst them are some of the Island's other business success stories including Paul Rudling, whose company SP Systems has recently won the Queen's Award for Export, and Mike Aikin, boss of Wightlink, one of the Island ferry operators. Every time I catch Nick's eye, we both silently wonder how we have got from that first night in Seaview to this event. It seems a miracle.

I can't taste the food, although I do find myself watching every single detail of the service. That's what being in the business does for you – even if you don't own the place you manage the function in your mind. With tickets at £150 a head, plus VAT, I wonder about their costings – who is getting the profit? I also wonder how the Grosvenor House would measure up against the Business Excellence model. Then I look up to see the empty stage with its three vast screens and lectern.

Throughout the dinner, I keep drifting off, thinking about earlier that day. Our trip round the *Daily Telegraph* offices and its archives, by invitation of Carole Dawson Young, the journalist who has written a feature on us that will appear in their business section later in the week. The amazing tour of the fiftieth floor of Canary Wharf, not even experienced by Tony Blair yet, with its crystal-clear view up to Windsor and out over the Dome to Southend. Then lunch at my old firm Corney & Barrow's latest wine bar in the new Docklands development, followed by an afternoon trying to calm down while being pestered by a reporter from the *Daily Mail*.

Suddenly the meal is over and the spectacle starts. First there are the speeches . . . on and on they go: excellence, strategy, process, resources, model facts and figures that I can't take in. Screens full of special promotional videos about each of the finalists. Slick shots, loud upbeat music, tremendous graphics, artful corporate images, marketing ploys which must have cost tens of thousand of pounds. The images portrayed on the screen confirm that we're outclassed and well out of our league. Each of the other finalists is looking confident that they will sweep the board. Sitting here in the middle with my family, I feel very gauche and like a pretender. By the time our video comes on, Nick and I really wonder if we're in the right room. Someone on the table behind giggles as Paul Burden, the BBC reporter from their Breakfast news business section, refers to us as 'faultless towers' – I want to curl up and die.

On the screen, there we are for all to see, our staff Charlie and Leon, Ali and Philippa, quietly and efficiently going about their work. Then Mary and Gill in housekeeping, shaking open freshly pressed white sheets. Tom, a young chef, preparing lunch while explaining why he enjoys working at the Seaview. Sarah in reception, talking about the importance of teamwork. Shots of the modern, new blue-and-white Sunshine Restaurant, and oranges cut in half and squeezed for breakfast. Then a sequence of pictures of Nick greeting and serving guests, and me talking to the staff. A straight-forward look at a small business. No hype or pretension. But Meridian Television, who kindly prepared the short video, edited from a programme they made about the Seaview, have done a good job. The little hotel on the Isle of Wight looks great up there on the silver screens.

After what seems an eternity, the gold envelopes are opened. There are three joint winners – BT Payphone, Nortel, and us. Nick and I rise from our seats and receive great applause, tears, hugs, the lot! The walk to the lectern seems to take ages, with people stopping to offer congratulations and shaking our hands. Finally we reach the stage. Speech in hand (I have three copies, just in case), I get out my new reading glasses. Trembling with nerves, I nearly poke my eye out and have to admit that I don't normally wear glasses but that my daughters have assured me they make me look more businesslike – a big laugh. Speech over, and clutching the huge and very heavy trophy, I'm blinded by flashing lights. Nick is right beside me, both of us exultant and feeling as important as stars. Well, we are stars, at least for a few seconds. More photos, more interviews.

Some time later, after all the glamour and glitter, we squash together in the tiny bed in my mother's flat in London, very proud. We've won.

The Seaview Hotel is a double-fronted building tucked away like a boat in harbour between two Georgian stone houses halfway down the village high street. The hotel's Edwardian façade conceals the fact that it was originally one of a series of private houses built by a Mr William Caws for his children in 1800. Side by side, the properties run down the high street towards the sea. Separating the Island from the mainland are the busy waters of the Solent, dotted with old forts built by Palmerston in 1860 to keep out the French. Across the sea lies the city of Portsmouth, steeped in naval history. Hovercraft, passenger and car ferries continuously speed across the six-mile strip of water, while larger ferries plough out past the forts, across the Channel to Cherbourg, Le Havre, Caen and St

Malo. Islands linked to islands linked to Europe.

Our first five years at the hotel were the hardest. There was plenty of scope for improvement – in fact we could only go up. If you can survive the first five years of a new business then you are going to make it, for sure. Our real difficulty, something faced by so many small businesses, was no cash. We had taken on a very seasonal business at the end of the season. The hotel had previously only been viable for a couple of months during the summer. Having taken out a huge mortgage to buy the hotel (double the maximum the bank had originally offered) we had nothing spare to spend on refurbishment. Each new plate, glass, knife, fork, coat hanger and box of tissues had to come out of profit after we had paid the bank. In the early 1980s interest rates suddenly soared. The capital from the sale of our house in London was quickly gobbled up. Our worried accountant described us as 'highly geared'. There was nowhere else to turn, the business had to fend for itself. It was then we worked on developing a particularly good relationship with our bank manager. We had to.

The other problem was that only four of the sixteen bedrooms had private bathrooms and some of the accommodation at the back of the hotel had only been used for staff. The carpets were thread-bare, bedspreads tatty candlewick, and every wall upstairs was covered in chip paper painted 'magnolia'. The entire infrastructure needed over-hauling. The front bar was made of plywood and much of the furniture was what can only be described as 'early MFI'. The dining room had red-and-gold 'tandoori' flock with contrasting squirly patterned carpet and the huge but grubby Sunshine Bar at the back had a cracked lino floor and a bad reputation.

During the initial five years, in spite of the arrival of our children Philippa, better known as Pip, and two years later Julia, called Jules, we worked ridiculous hours. We hardly ever took time off. (Between contractions, while in hospital for the birth of Jules, I was caught by a horrified midwife, pushing ten-pence coins into a phone box while explaining to Nick in the hotel kitchen exactly how to prepare Mrs Thursfield's 'special' chicken dish for her regular ladies' bridge luncheon party.) Nick asked me to cook for the first six weeks until we employed a chef. Unfortunately, it took over six years to find one, and then only because I was forced out of the kitchen by ill health. When I returned I discovered that the young lads I had trained had done extremely well in my absence, so I let them take over with only limited supervision from me. Since then they have gone from strength to strength and one, Charlie, is running the kitchen today. We set our course and stuck with it.

My mother, a hotelier herself, had taught me that the secret to a successful hotel is 'bottoms in beds'. Every empty bedroom or unlet restaurant table is a business loss. How could we attract people to Seaview other than in August? Who wants to come to a sailing village in November, when there are no boats? We were only two hours' drive from central

London, so we thought we must be able to attract some of that huge market. But how exactly to get the bottoms in beds was the challenge.

Food could be a start. In the early eighties, the recent British culinary revolution had just begun. The Roux brothers still owned their original small restaurant, Le Gavroche, in Pimlico, and Chez Nico had only just started in Battersea. Out in the provinces Brown Windsor or mulligatawny were the soup of the day and Birds Eye frozen peas reigned supreme. At Corney & Barrow we had supplied wine to many of the new young chefs, Alastair Little at his first restaurant in Putney and, in the West Country, a little-known self-trained chef who was enthusiastic about local produce and fish, Rick Stein. Nick at the Athenaeum had hosted special dinners prepared by John Tovey, owner of the Miller Howe hotel in the Lake District, with his great friend Delia Smith.

Nick and I took with us our passion for food and wine. We wanted to share that with our customers at an economical price. So off the menu went frozen halibut steaks with mixed frozen veg and on came fresh local sea bass with seakale grown on the Seaview allotment. It was the food that would attract the new business, especially from London. I rolled up my sleeves and took charge in the kitchen. Drawing on my schooling in the culinary arts from a young age in my father's hotel kitchen, I knew to concentrate on fresh Island produce, simply but deliciously presented. At that time the Island had the best crab, lobster, prawns, oysters and mussels.

(Tragically, the extensive oyster and mussel beds were ruined by anti-fouling chemicals used on boats during the eighties). Local farms produced delicious spring lamb, beef, pork, venison, pheasant, tomatoes, asparagus, early new potatoes, broccoli, soft fruit (especially raspberries and straw-berries) and even their own garlic. There were two vineyards, both producing white wines, at Adgestone and Barton Manor.

In those days it was difficult to get interesting and varied ingredients. I returned to the London barrow boys near where I used to live in Chelsea to collect huge bags of oak-leaf lettuce, radicchio, passion fruit and mangos. All of which were impossible to find outside the capital. I soon learnt to use my imagination; there are countless things you can do with carrots or parsnips, especially with the latest invention at the time, the Magimix. I worked directly with the Island farmers to fulfil the restaurant's requirements and we grew our own herbs in a small walled garden outside our house, Jasmine Cottage, next to the hotel. Fresh, fresh, fresh was the word. A grey mullet caught a couple of hours earlier from the muddy Bembridge harbour was preferable to a piece of turbot that had spent too long on a slab in Grimsby. Beautiful fresh flat fish, like plaice and lemon sole, were lightly grilled whole on the bone and served simply with a knob of parsley butter. Seaview lobster served cold in their shells with salad, chips and thick, rich home-made mayonnaise. My favourite restaurant in London, and one of my best wine accounts, had been Daphne's in Draycott Avenue, South Kensington. I brought with me their rack of lamb with minted hollandaise and made it my own.

As the food for grown-ups improved, we didn't fail to provide suitable food for the children. Using our experience as parents of three young children, we provided an interesting and appetising high-tea menu complete with boiled eggs, Marmite toast or soldiers. With success in the restaurant, overnight guests followed.

Any new hotelier quickly discovers that breakfast has to be every bit as good as the evening meal. After all, you can't rely on wine to smoothe out the rough edges after badly cooked eggs or slow service at eight o'clock in the morning. One of the best ways for a young chef to start his training and pick up basic culinary skills is to work on the many different and delicate dishes prepared with an egg, as Delia was to teach us all years later. We worked on our poached, boiled, scrambled and fried. Unlike many rural hotels at that time, we happily cooked early breakfast for businessmen before they had to go off to their first appointment. We also kept the kitchens open late at night and prepared a proper meal for the late arrival, rather than offering cold sandwiches in the bedroom.

Catering to each guest's individual needs was another key to our success. Everyone who worked with us had to be completely focused on trying to make each and every person who entered our doors happy at all times. This is, of course, impossible in practice but a worthy target to aim for. Now, after the first two years, the 'bottoms in beds' began to keep coming back.

Another aspect of the business we needed to develop was a local following. At the time, we were the only pub in the village. Nick and I had limited experience as innkeepers and the first couple of years were a steep learning curve. In particular we had to become the local landlord and landlady. We revived the village darts team and joined the area league. The team swiftly became known as the Seaview SODS. Seaview 'Otel Darts Squad. Once a week the motley band, including landlord and landlady and led by Reg Orlandini, a local journalist and cartoonist, would either set off to another Island pub or stay in Seaview for a home match. Licensing hours were extended by members of the team checking into the hotel so they could legally buy late-night drinks as residents. It was fortuitous that the bedrooms above were empty because a rendition of 'On the Banks of the River' by Willie Caws, the local builder, would ring up through the floorboards. We rarely got to bed before 2am. It was a very silly and rowdy period in the hotel's history and we ended up being forced out of the league after numerous complaints about the SODS' bad behaviour. Arriving at pubs singing Christmas carols in October was frowned upon, as was dressing up as schoolboys, in shorts. Mooning the opposition before the start of play was the last straw. The East Wight Darts League threw us out and the SODS disbanded during the winter of 1984. That era of the hotel's history disappeared, except for Reg Orlandini's original cartoon still hanging on the wall in the public bar.

Following this phase of raucous play and late-night drinking the pub at the Seaview began to change. The stained and sodden carpets, glaring lights and fruit machines, were banished and replaced with subtle light from ship lanterns, stripped wooden decking, old oars, broken masts, lobster pots and a huge, wooden, ship's wheel. The ghastly modern gas fire was chucked out and the original open stone fireplace re-established, giving off a warm red glow from the burning embers on winter nights.

Meanwhile, the smarter residents' bar at the front of the hotel was transformed, to reappear looking rather like a room from a gentlemen's club. We built a new, solid mahogany bar and painted the walls deep red and navy before covering them with pictures of boats. On one wall hundreds of black-and-white photographs of classic naval ships, HMS *Nelson* steaming through the Atlantic with the home fleet, HMS *King George V* in Sydney harbour, HMS *Devonshire* returning the King of Denmark to Copenhagen, and details of the *Hood* and *Rodney*. Up by the bar I framed a series of caricatures of naval officers named after drinks: Pink Gin, Large Port and Gin & It. On the opposite wall photographs, postcards and menus from the great liners were added to two framed receipts for instalment payments on the *Queen Mary* and *Queen Elizabeth*. Just outside the bar, above a photograph of the *Titanic* off Ireland, is a copy of an extraordinary letter. Written by Eileen, a nine-year-old passenger on board the fatal liner, it details the start of the maiden voyage of the 'biggest ship in the world', its swimming pool, gym and Turkish bath, how it is due into Cherbourg at five but she thinks it will be late. It was donated by a regular customer, like so much of the maritime collection. We were all relieved to discover that Eileen disembarked in France before the tragic Atlantic crossing.

Combining the new-look bars with the excellent locally brewed ale and a new range of delicious pub meals, all at really inexpensive prices, put our bars and food on the map. One lesson we learnt in all this was how important it was to attract a wider local trade from all over the Island and just across the water too. This is still a crucial aspect of our business today.

As the revenue from the bar, restaurant and accommodation began to rise in tandem, we had the capital to invest in a more complete refurbishment of the hotel.

This coincided with that expansive period in the history of tourism when the package deal first arrived and people started taking their main holiday abroad and enjoying the delights of the new modern facilities in Spain, Italy and later the whole Mediterranean. En suite had become *de rigueur*. Business people returned from conferences around the world and raved about the perfection of American or Far Eastern service. Suddenly, we were all part of the hospitality industry. Back in Britain, on family holidays or short business trips, no one now wanted to pad down a corridor in slippers and dressing gown to a shared bathroom. The upgrading had to be done, and every alteration required major investment. As quickly as the hotel made money by attracting new business, every penny became a means of ensuring that guests would return.

First we had to rewire and replumb the whole building. The immediate benefit was that the building was no longer a serious fire risk and the new copper pipes ran clear rather than dirty brown water from the bath taps. Anyone taking on new premises will soon discover that the replacement of an old or inadequate hidden infrastructure will be one of the greatest expenses. If it is not replaced immediately the problem will not go away but only get worse.

Then came private bathrooms, the en suites. How do you turn bedrooms without bathrooms into bedrooms *with* bathrooms? Well, you lose bedrooms. That is why you won't find a bedroom numbered 8, 11 or 14 at the Seaview. But the business couldn't afford to lose the accommodation revenue, so once we had added the bathrooms we then extended at the back of the hotel, building more bedrooms, to end up with a total of sixteen.

While we modernised the hotel we also personalised it, stamping it with our own particular taste. Out went harsh overhead lighting, in came low lamps with dimmers. Saggy beds were replaced with top-of-the-range, expensive, interior-sprung mattresses to give a better night's sleep. Unlined cheap curtains gave way to rich, thick, long drapes with matching bedspreads and cushions. Nasty matchstick furniture was replaced with family antiques. We filled all the rooms with our own large collection of interesting books for both adults and children. New modern electrical appliances became standard in every room and then we added a few extras of our own. Now standard items in quality hotels, we provided bottles of mineral water, individual hand-made pincushions for needlework, watercolour picture postcards of the hotel, writing paper and envelopes and biscuits made from flour ground at a local mill in Calbourne in the west of the Island.

The original hotel restaurant was spruced up with white linen and silver, fresh flowers and smart candle lights with navy shades. People like to see into restaurants, so the doors and a large section of the wall along the corridor were glass. Everyone knew who was dining at the Seaview.

We also invested extensively in staff training, including ourselves. Knowing that we didn't have a luxurious, country-house hotel set in idyllic sur-roundings meant we needed to be professional, efficient, welcoming and constantly trying to give more. This attitude of always trying to give the highest standards had to be passed on to each employee. Recruiting Islanders was hard: our industry had a terrible reputation and most locals entering catering found themselves employed in summer and unemployed by winter. There was little encouragement for young people to train in an industry notorious for long weary hours and appalling pay. It was just something you did to fill in time before you got a proper job. Gradually, working with the Isle of Wight college of further education, and with Island schools, we tried to change that perception.

Right from the very start, we sent our young employees off to experience top-quality 'role model' establishments like John Tovey's hotel, the Miller Howe in Windermere, the old L'Ecu de France in Jermyn Street, Claridge's and the Connaught, so they could know what to aspire to. We encouraged chefs who visited us, like Michel Bourdin from the Connaught, to allow our young chefs to watch their kitchens in action – in the Connaught's case a multi-million-pound, very classy kitchen. I regularly went to London to train and learn from others, returning to train in-house, with new approaches to ingredients and new dishes. Following a course I attended with Anton Mosimann, two fellow members of the course, young Australian chefs, came and worked with us that summer, bringing with them the exciting new food combinations then popular in the southern hemisphere, combining classic European with the delights of the Far East.

As the national attitude to training changed we enthusiastically followed the new trends and applied for the respected training award, Investors in People. We took on 'modern apprentices' and ensured all our chefs gained the standard National Vocational Qualification level 3, as well as their extensive in-house training. Every member of staff has his or her own profile file containing their appraisal forms and training certificates, so they can see how they're progressing and have improved, along with details of any disciplinary procedures. We took on the role of training and once employees were qualified we watched many of them go off and succeed all over the world.

As the years went by, we embraced environmentally friendly policies, recycling our wine bottles, installing low-voltage lights, reusing old menus and paper, and sourcing products and produce through the village shop. The benefits of this hard-won self-sufficiency were surprising. Clearing bottles in our normal rubbish cost money; the recycling bins were emptied for free. The investment in training resulted in higher-quality service and low staff turnover. Money was saved on heat, light and other power bills. In fact, there were savings all round.

Nick and I have always run the hotel as a partnership, with shared responsibility from the whole team. It soon became clear that everyone who worked at Seaview wanted each guest to have a unique and memorable experience and feel surprised at the amount of five-star de luxe pampering they enjoyed at a very affordable price. Training our own managers and promoting within the team created commitment and dedication to the business.

We recruit many different people, of all ages, often with limited hotel experience but a positive and pleasant attitude. They soon develop a clear understanding of the ethos of the Seaview and, backed by sound training, they grow to their full potential before moving on. We take the view that energetic and ambitious employees will naturally want to move on but most choose to remain and grow within the hotel.

At breakfast, Philippa reigns supreme, welcoming down the early risers as the smell of fresh coffee and bacon permeates the hotel. She came to us after living an interesting and varied life, with a will and charm of her own. David also came to us after years in the merchant navy. He runs the restaurant, greeting each diner by name after checking what he refers to as his passenger list. Having a wide range of ages and backgrounds gives the staff its strength. Ali came to the Seaview in 1983. Born in Kenya, with roots in Pakistan, his tall, noble stature and wisdom spread calm through the busy kitchen. He not only runs the indispensable team responsible for washing and cleaning everything, but supervises the ordering of supplies; moreover, he has a natural capacity to guide and support the younger members. All the older members are good at looking after and settling down some of the younger employees, while the under-25s have a better grasp of the new technology than Nick and me. All this leads to a balanced and happy workforce.

Every Friday, at 10am, we hold a meeting to look at individual departments and up-and-coming events which affect the entire hotel. The main five hotel departments – restaurant, bedrooms, kitchen, bar and office – send one or two representatives to the meeting. It is a very important time to sort out exactly what has happened and is going to happen.

Every employee is invited to try out the hotel's restaurant and managers stay as guests to assess the quality and service. Comments, criticisms and suggestions, from employees and guests alike, are all fed back into the weekly meeting to benefit the whole team. During the week any problems are reported in a manager's book, like a ship's log, and this is all discussed on a Friday.

Nick and I, with help from our accountant and bank manager, draw up short- and long-term business and training plans and budgets. The budgets give different departments clear targets and weekly figures act as an incentive. Though we strive for improvement in both room occupancy and restaurant covers, especially during the low season, this is carefully juggled with the needs and expectations of guests. It is, for example, important not to get so busy that the hotel's high standards fall.

Once a month the figures are discussed in detail. We look not only at the turnover but also, more important, the wages bill as a percentage of turnover and the figures between departments, compared with those in the same month on previous years. Angela, in the hotel office, prepares simple colour graphs and pie charts which are pinned up on the department noticeboards, so everyone can see how they are doing.

While Nick and I know we need to constantly refurbish and upgrade the business, in terms of the hotel's assets our staff welfare is our priority. With every single person's views and options valued, we don't just *say* they are our best asset, we know and believe it. Each department has an input to both planning the hotel refurbishment and the purchase of capital equipment, along with other suggestions for their own benefit. Should we have a hotel pension scheme or employee saving fund? Nick and I believe that by training, valuing and supporting everyone at the Seaview, we ensure that they value, support and professionally care for the guests. This is shown to be working by the constant stream of positive feedback we get about all our staff.

New employees are given careful induction, regular assessment with their training, and everyone, including Nick and I, is appraised twice yearly. As parents ourselves, we like to invite the parents of young employees either for free meals or reduced rates on accommodation so they can see for themselves what we do at the Seaview and also how we train and care for our employees. From the very start, we needed local staff accommodation because of poor public transport. Initially, we rented a small flat just up the road from the hotel, above Caws shoe shop, but eventually we managed to purchase our own flat which can accommodate at least four live-in staff. We also recruited a number of local families who could lodge summer students. Staff facilities, breaks, meals and accommodation are all considered very important.

Support and counselling are on offer for those with difficulties. Naturally as the workforce grew, so life presented some small (or sometimes tragic) problems which none of us wanted any member of the team to have to cope with alone. If staff were to be happy and thoughtful towards our guests, we needed to ensure that each member of the team was reasonably happy in life. In 1992 I qualified with RSA Counselling and Learning Skills and in 1995 graduated from Portsmouth University with a diploma in Counselling.

While sincerely believing that the people working at the Seaview are its greatest resource, we also know they are the highest cost. Staff rotas constantly have to be carefully monitored with holidays and time off slotted in around quiet periods. Students and part-time staff are taken on for busy periods, reducing costs off season. This is why, in such a labour-intensive industry, the wages bill is meticulously checked against turnover every week.

We developed, over many years, a detailed list of the names and addresses of our regular guests who wish to be sent details of special promotions. Every week the pie charts showed how nearly half of our business was repeat or personal recommendation by regular customers. It was vital to stay in contact with regulars, encouraging them back with special reductions, particularly off season.

Nick and I have always worked 'hands on', running, monitoring and fine-tuning the business, while working on improving our own skills. Nick works predominantly 'front of house', not only welcoming guests at the door and individually seeing each guest before they leave, but also taking an active role in all bookings, overseeing each department, particularly the restaurant, including all stock and financial controls and staff and customer liaisons. He is very much an old-fashioned *patron*.

I supervise the kitchen and menus, working with the chefs, trying to create innovative new dishes. But I also concentrate on organising staff training, welfare and recruitment. Nick and I work together on future planning, budgets, promotions, refurbishment and new building projects (though he gives me a free hand with most designs). I spend hours, when not reading cookery books, selecting my own interior designs suitable to the business and building.

Every bedroom has a customer's comment form, with space to add suggestions and report faults. When guests check out we specifically ask how they enjoyed their stay, trying to establish if there was any way we could improve the service. Any problems or difficulties are dealt with immediately and reported in the log at reception, ready for the weekly meeting.

Every guest who completes a form or writes to praise or criticise the hotel in any way, receives a personal letter from us thanking them for taking the trouble. Specific details or complaints are dealt with in the letter and if we take up their suggestion we always write back to let them know. We realised early on that guests love to feel part of the operation. Like many of the employees, they had brilliant suggestions and their complaints enabled us to improve and raise our standards. All feedback is good and can be used to improve your business.

With only one small restaurant, we had to have two sittings. Some guests didn't wish to dine late, and others didn't like cigarette smoke. Building the second restaurant meant we could offer every guest the time they wanted and a choice of smoking or non-smoking. There are two non-smoking bedrooms, introduced after one guest with breathing difficulties particularly wanted to avoid the smell of stale cigarettes.

Traditional hotel problems, such as a lack of understanding between kitchen and restaurant staff, are dealt with immediately. Because members from every department job-swop regularly with other departments, and then bring back their experience to the Friday meeting, these hardly ever occur. Problems and difficulties are discussed with heads of department so that even if immediate action is not possible everyone is made aware.

Regular visits to other pubs and restaurants to 'taste' and learn also provide an 'off the job' ambience in which problems can be discussed in a relaxed atmosphere. It is really important to sort out problems and difficulties in a small business – they can quickly grow and be very destructive.

At the same time as running the hotel, from the very start Nick and I took an active role in Seaview village life. Apart from using the village shops, we also help organise and support village events throughout the year. We work closely with the local primary school at Nettlestone, which was attended by Pip and Jules. Whole classes visit the hotel and we are currently helping to sponsor them to participate in the Investors in People award.

When in 1998 the British Quality Foundation team sent in their detailed report we were all delighted to see they had highlighted the Seaview's strengths, giving particular emphasis to, 'team working' with 'excellent leadership', our 'deeply rooted customer focus' and 'simple, non bureaucratic management', the 'deeply felt staff loyalty' and our focus on 'training and development' within a 'supportive culture' that did not lack a 'firm approach when needed'. When looking for areas for improvement, they said they found no major issues, but simply urged us to continue prioritising our customers' needs and to extend our IT skills so that we could improve our ability to analyse results. After a long nerve-racking wait for this 'school report' we were all thrilled.

So at the end of October, glowing with pride, we braced ourselves for another winter of continued improvement.

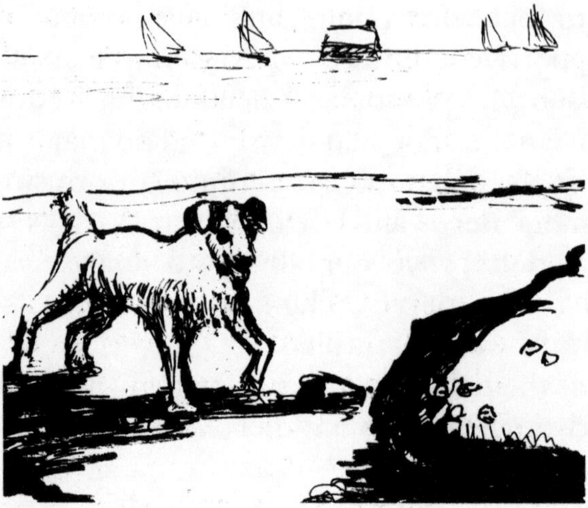

CHAPTER 2

NOVEMBER
Nagging the Nag

With the onset of November all the boats have been put away and the winter field sports start. Heads turn from the empty and grey sea to the land, rich with autumn colours. Days get shorter and amber nights close in. Unexpected easterly storms can result in the Island being temporarily cut off from the south coast of England, which in rough weather is no longer visible beyond the forts. We can become a community marooned. Though never for long, as the sturdy car ferries manage to struggle across in all weathers. The cosy intimacy of the Seaview becomes a lovely haven against the vagaries of oncoming winter.

Business in November is unpredictable at the hotel. Normally it is fairly quiet, but not this year. Figures are up, room occupancy and restaurant covers are exceptionally good. This may be thanks to media coverage which followed in the wake of our winning the award. Television, radio and newspapers, both national and local, the trade press, even the financial pages of the *Daily Telegraph*, all gave the hotel a tremendous write-up.

A problem with running a small seasonal hotel is maintaining continuity in the winter. The people who work at the hotel, its vital ingredients, come together during the peak period and perform like the well-rehearsed cast of a play. But if they all leave at the end of the summer season you have no players for the winter, and no continuity for the following year.

Knowing that this year we achieved so much, our problem is going to be how to keep standards up to expectations. Our good employment practices, while making perfect business sense, need a healthy turnover all year round. The problem, of course, is that there can be some very quiet times in the winter. With nearly forty staff to pay weekly, and look after, November can be a long and worrying month if the customers are not there. Our first November, we had six employees and two guests: one a construction engineer called Howard Fine, who was working on building a new power station at East Cowes, the other a Mrs Mathius, a delightful elderly lady, who was blind and had an infuriatingly loud hearing aid which constantly buzzed. Each night Nick would shout out the evening menu to her alone in the dining room before Howard came back for a late supper. If anyone else came to dine, Nick had to explain loudly exactly who had joined Mrs Mathius in the restaurant.

Many Novembers later, in 1996, after the stock market crash and Black Wednesday, we knew we were facing a downturn in the economy; and, for us, a very long, hard winter.

We had reinvested heavily earlier that year,

building the new Sunshine Restaurant, named after the Sunshine Bar that was there before. To serve the new restaurant we had to completely refurbish the kitchens. Still compact at only thirty-three feet by fourteen, they were now steel-clad from floor to ceiling and boasted a new extraction system and non-slip floor. We installed a complete new range and built an external walk-in fridge and freezer. It was like a gleaming engine room, where in August, when the pressure was up, the seven chefs would steam away like stokers. With the constant flow of the waiting staff on a busy night, it became a hubbub of activity – orders arrive, details are shouted out to those concerned, and each dish is carefully prepared.

With the depressing long-term economic forecast of 1996, we had to quickly come up with an idea for that winter. We decided to offer free accommodation to our regular customers, who would only have to pay for their food and drink. What we needed were hedonistic alcoholics and over-eaters. Luckily everyone who came had vociferous appetites, and while wining and dining they also discovered how lovely Seaview could be out of season, with its long, deserted beach walks and roaring open fire in the locals' bar. Now many return regularly each winter to enjoy the special winter breaks we offer. This, combined with additional media coverage over the last two winters, the result of winning the Meridian and then the UK award, has clearly had a very positive effect. Winter occupancy has risen dramatically compared with 1995.

The new November menus are in place; and include the first local pheasants, their prices settled by much barter and negotiation with the game-keeper. (We'll settle prices for the first spring lobster catch in the same way.) For the last couple of seasons we have had a good supply of pheasant from one of the larger shoots in the centre of the Island. These birds really are free-range. They come in by the brace and are hung for no more than two days – we never serve game particularly high, because it's not popular. Their feathers and innards are removed and the birds prepared by the chefs, using the delicate breast meat only, the remainder going to make game stock and soup. We lightly sear the breast meat with fresh sage from the garden, wrap it in bacon and roast it in the oven. It's served on an apple, bacon and sage mash with a rich *jus* made from a reduction of the game stock. Followed by a good winter dessert like hot roasted pears with ginger ice cream.

The boys in the kitchen slowly work their way through the various holidays. It is always hard when a key member of staff is on leave, as the others have to cover all his or her shifts, and it is particularly hard for the kitchen in November when the restaurant numbers vary enormously day to day. Nobody can predict what will happen – one Sunday we may be half empty for lunch and the next they'll be hanging from the rafters. In the summer, when we know the numbers are likely to be high, we increase staff numbers accordingly, but in November it is less easy to forecast and you can be caught off guard. We don't have part-time staff in reserve that we can call in.

Much planning is going on upstairs. We have to decide which rooms are to be completely redecorated, and exactly what we want to do: what colours, alterations and fabrics we need and how much we want to spend. Those bedrooms that are not being redecorated over the course of the winter will be spring-cleaned. While most things in the hotel are bought locally, I go to London to get all our new material from John Lewis and Peter Jones. Initially I tried many other suppliers both on the Island as well as the famous fabric suppliers in London, but whenever I compared wholesale prices John Lewis came out ahead. Even at retail prices nobody offered such a wide range of good-quality fire-resistant fabrics in imaginative designs. More importantly, they quickly and cheaply deliver to the Isle of Wight and the assistants don't look at me as though I am asking for something to be sent to Outer Mongolia. Later, I was offered a trade discount based on the amount we purchased. We must be a good advertisement for them as guests constantly ask where we find all the different fabrics.

This year we have to buy new materials for the restaurant at the front of the hotel. We were meant to start work in November but, as a result of the extra bookings, we decided to delay until early January instead. So planning is under way, with the choice of fabric difficult because our longest-standing customers like the tradition of the old décor. But many who have experienced the bright blue colours in the Sunshine Restaurant at the rear will expect something spectacular in the revamping of the front restaurant. We always make a conscious effort to ensure there is a visible change on the ground floor every year, so that when guests return they can immediately see what we have done with their money. We are often asked who does the interior design. As in the kitchen department, I have no formal design training and only took on the role because we simply couldn't afford an expensive designer. Now, after years of experience, I wander round Terence Conran's shops and restaurants soaking up ideas. Most of all, I like to see the latest restaurants in any metropolis I visit – London, Edinburgh or Barcelona.

The lighting is all-important: it can totally change the atmosphere of a room. For eighteen years at the Seaview we have used the same firm of electricians, who by now know every wire and junction in the place. But we have had our share of problems, near disasters even. When we first bought the hotel the entire place needed rewiring. The two young electricians, both called Mike, from Berry & Kitchen, were a dream come true, and, in spite of our financial restrictions, somehow got it sorted. We then went on to expand and add to the system, but it was never simple. One area where we scored highly with the awards assessors was our economical use of energy sources. This frugality wasn't, I have to admit, always out of choice. We would have happily used commercial three-phase power in the hotel if it had been possible to install within a reasonable budget. It never was. The nearest supply was at the top of the hill; to bring it down to the hotel was going to cost £10,000. At that price we made do with the small domestic supply we had inherited. Now, nearly twenty years on, we are applauded for our economical use of power. But not having a three-phase system when you are running a commercial establishment causes terrible problems.

The consequence of having a domestic supply are that we are not able to install any industrial equipment like a commercial dishwashing machine. We did manage to install the in-house laundry, but had to have all the machines converted to work on two-phase. There is also a limit to how much refrigeration and air-conditioning we could install and run at the same time.

We added individual Dimplex convection heaters to all our bedrooms, but then had to remove some and extend the gas central heating following one cold New Year's Eve when the entire hotel was plunged into darkness in the middle of a festive dinner. Every guest had turned their heater on full. Needless to say, one of the two Mikes arrived like the cavalry and power was restored within the hour. We later discovered the hotel fuse box had nearly melted. Hardly any of the guests noticed. We just lit more candles and they thought we had turned the lights down on purpose. They were quite happy, but I was trying to cook and going mad. Have you ever tried to serve up sixty gastronomic delights in a steaming kitchen by candlelight? After that, we made a point of inviting one of the electricians to join us for a free New Year's Eve – just in case.

In November we traditionally hold the first of our winter wine tastings. This is part of our plans to encourage those who only know Seaview as a summer delight to discover its off-season charms – and keep us in business. My years in the wine trade with Corney & Barrow still pay dividends and we have loyally continued to support them here on the Island, my old boss Richard Peat coming down each year to hold an autumn tasting. To complement the wines, we lay on a special dinner when some of the vintages from the tasting are served with the meal. Over the years, this basic format has developed and now other wine merchants also hold tastings and give lectures at the Seaview, throughout the year. These have become a regular attraction for a certain number of our clientele. This time the season of tastings has extended even further and the last one will be in June, just as the new potatoes start, the asparagus finishes and the lobsters are at their best.

For this November tasting I have tried a rather unusual menu. It includes Steak and Kidney with a West Country suet cake. I know it is an odd dish for a wine tasting, and rather a gamble, but I think it will work with the rich and full-bodied wines Richard has chosen. We don't want things to become boring.

1998 WINTER WINE TASTING

Thursday 19th November 1998

Richard Peat from Corney & Barrow
presenting a selection of wines
followed by dinner

Hot Leek Mousse with Lobster & Shellfish Sauce

Kushushu Creek Chardonnay, Robertson 1997

Steak & Kidney cooked in Guinness with
home-made West Country Suet Cake

Pinot Noir, Vieilles Vignes, Cattin 1996

Mr Minghella's Rich Vanilla Ice Cream
with Amaretto liqueur & Biscuit

Fresh Coffee with Island cream & mints

Cossart Gordon 5-year-old Boal

Total price £27.50
per person including VAT @ 17.5%
including the tasting, dinner & all dinner wines

Slight and eccentric, dressed in a velvet jacket
with monogrammed velvet slippers, Richard Peat is
a past master at events like these. His customers
include the brilliant wine buyers from the many
Oxford and Cambridge colleges and specialised
restaurateurs like Rick Stein. He spins little
anecdotes while passing on his vast knowledge of
oenology in an amusing and informative manner. A

true wine-trade legend, like much of old Corney &
Barrow, he is part of another era when working in
wine was considered the only 'trade' suitable for a
young man of breeding. Richard's family was part
of the famous firm of accountants, Peat, Marwick &
Mitchell, but his true love had always been wine.
Lafite and Bâtard-Montrachet fascinated him and,
having been a devoted customer he went on to join
the board of Corney & Barrow. He was a delightful
boss and I was privileged to work in the City during
a fascinating era. On his annual visits, Richard
helps Nick resculpt our wine list and keeps us
informed on the latest happenings in the trade. This
year he tells us the 1998 vintage is looking good.
We soak up the wine-trade gossip and his numerous
tips, ready to pass them on to our interested
customers.

November also brings a visit from Paul
Whittome, one of the founder members and a
driving force behind the Great Inns of England. We
first came in contact with Paul a few years ago,
while visiting Nick's brother Tim in Norfolk; we
were so impressed with his business, the Hoste
Arms in Burnham Market, that we agreed to join
their informal group of like-minded establishments.
Recently Nick felt that we needed to be under the
umbrella of a larger group after more than fifteen
years on our own. Being fiercely independent, I
wanted to maintain our individuality. The benefit
of joining this particular group is that it gives us
many of the advantages of a larger organisation but
still allows us to maintain our unique style and

independence. That's the theory, anyway, and Nick assures me it's true.

We have a jolly dinner with Paul and his charming wife, who pass on lots of useful tips for us in every field of the business. In particular, we are interested in how they recently bought an old station house just down the road from the Hoste, now called the Railway Inn, which they use as an overflow. This is one thing we desperately need at the Seaview. They have only been running the Hoste Arms for five years but in that time they have expanded more than we have in almost twenty. It's an impressive story and we both feel fired with enthusiasm. The Whittomes tell us about a company called 'Loos with a View'. After they leave, I log on to their web site and spend hours exploring the range of stylish and clever clear perspex loo seats filled with things like jellybeans or barbed wire, spiders or sea horses. They are such brilliant novelties we decide to drive up to their head office just off the M25 and M3 to collect a selection of clear blue seats brimming like rock pools with crabs, shells, fish and seaweed. I know they will be a great source of amusement to many guests, especially the younger ones. At well over £100 a seat we can't afford them for every room, but we get six to start with and will see how they go.

Twenty-seven nine- and ten-year-olds from Class 4 at Nettlestone, the local primary school, are due to visit the 'award-winning hotel' today. They are setting off from the school on the green at Nettlestone at 10am to walk down the hill to

Seaview. Is everything ready? The staff are all pre-pared. School visits and work experience are very important. A child's impression today may stick with him or her and later affect a career choice. There is a shocking skills shortage in the hospitality industry. We need to encourage youngsters to want to train to become chefs and receptionists. At the same time, it is a very positive experience for our employees, explaining to the children exactly what they do. Dividing the pupils with their teachers into three groups, Philippa and David from the restaurant and Charlie from the kitchen are due to show them round the whole hotel, answering their questions and pointing out how it all works.

Willie Caws, the local builder, whose great great grandfather William Caws built the hotel, is coming in later to give them a brief history of the village and the building of the hotel. I have made up special packs of information with all the details. Then we have laid on drinks, home-made chocolate brownies and hot choux puffs. We know that these children will be very honest with us if things are not up to scratch. Their assessment of the hotel will be almost as important, long term, as the BQF assessors'.

I am trying to avoid the children's goodies as I'm on a diet, which is going well, as long as I don't have to taste anything. Mr Minghella, supplier of the Island's ice cream (and father of the Oscar-winning film-director), called last night to see if we had tried his new blackcurrant sorbet. I didn't like to tell him I hadn't because I was trying to lose weight. It's such a problem in this industry. I just love food, with the inevitable consequences. Working long hours from early in the morning to late at night can mean that meals are missed and then, with a combination of low blood sugar and hunger, I eat far too much of the wrong food at the wrong time.

School visit over. All went well. The children loved the hot chocolate brownies and lemonade with a cherry. One little girl announced that she was 'definitely having her wedding here', so we have our first booking for the spring of 2010. They have now disappeared in a long crocodile, back up the hill with their packs of information and full tummies.

For part of this month Nick is away sailing with my brother and fellow hotelier, William, so I am left holding the fort. We seem to have had a spate of one-night bookings at weekends. I'm not too sure if we should hold hard to the policy of two nights or if I should let some of the rooms go. The problem is that with only sixteen rooms and full occupancy most weekends, if we let rooms for just Saturday night, then they lie empty on Friday, with the inevitable loss of revenue at a difficult time of year. It's funny how Nick and I work together, constantly chatting things through and verifying what each other knows and does; right and left brain working on separate details. With him away I'm not too sure I can function in the area where his head usually is.

Horror. A family of guests return covered in wet cement as a result of leaning on the village sea wall, which is currently being repaired by contractors from the council. They are not happy. What can I do? I phone the council and pass on to the guests the name of the Highway office but our local builder doesn't think they will get much satisfaction. The guests seem to think they can claim from the council. They leave the hotel armed with all relevant information, ready to pursue the matter once they get home.

One morning I glance up to discover a huge cobweb in the front restaurant at breakfast; spring-cleaning may come early this year. I've pointed it out to the breakfast staff, who must think I'm a terrible nag. I'm sorry, but it is exactly that kind of attention to detail everyone needs to spot. You have always to imagine what the guest will think if they spot something unsightly or out of place. But sometimes when I find myself nagging obsessively, I know it's time to take a break. I take the day off and drive out to Brighstone Forest on the west of the Island, in our old horse box, to ride our gentle black mare, Abby. We're accompanied by our two rescue dogs, Cleo, now nearly thirteen, who has been fed a steady diet of left-over fillet steak since we collected her from the RSPCA in 1987 when she was less than two, and Millie, a very naughty Jack Russell who has not mastered the art of good customer care and sometimes wants to evict our best guests. I find talking to Abby and the dogs incredibly relaxing, especially with Nick away. The animals don't mind if I nag.

Our manager, Leon, covering for Nick in his absence, is up until 3am with the two guests who want to drink late. Thank goodness he has the following day off and can catch up on his sleep. We never encourage late-night drinking as we have learnt over the years it normally causes problems and can easily result in other guests being disturbed.

I'm worried that bar items are not being properly charged to the rooms. Twice in one week, bar drinks have been left off bills. The mistakes are entered in the report book and taken to the weekly meeting for discussion.

I'm trying to chase up Mrs James, the brilliant seamstress from Nettlestone who makes all our curtains and bedspreads, about the new velvet undercovers for the Sunshine Restaurant tables. For some reason, she has only finished half and I know it will make a big difference when every table has a new, thick, blue velvet undercloth. I expect she is confused because we put back the redecoration of the old restaurant until January. I must call her to sort this out.

I check on the Christmas menus going out. By mid November we don't seem to be getting many function bookings and I wonder if it is because the menus we are offering are not quite right. Local firms telephone and ask for sample menus when planning their Christmas parties. The bookings are a vital part of our December trade. This year there is far more competition. My brother William bought the Royal, a former Trust House Forte hotel in Ventnor on the south of the Island, and over the last four years has gradually restored it to its former Victorian glory. Now the beautiful Appuldurcombe Restaurant, named after one of the Island's most famous and grand houses, has been designed by my sister Annie Dawes and recently matched us by gaining two AA rosettes for the food. At Yarmouth the historic George Hotel has had major reinvestment, and its chef Kevin Mangeolles is offering some of the best food on the Island. Closer to home, Biskra Beach, a hotel on the front at Ryde, has had an enormous investment from a Bahrain bank and now offers excellent accommodation and food. Closer still, and only half a mile down the road, an old priory was recently taken over by Andrew Palmer, former head of the New Covent Garden Soup Company. For years this rambling priory was a downmarket hostel for school parties, but now Andrew is quickly turning it into a beautiful country house hotel. In the long term, all this major investment is excellent for the Island, as is the eight million recently invested by Rank at the Bembridge Coastal Hotel. But it is bound to have an effect on the Seaview and will, of course, keep us on our toes. So competition for Christmas parties is keen this year.

Jill, who looks after the hotel garden and all the tubs and boxes, comes in to work. It looks so pretty since she took over the position of part-time gardener. It costs more to employ a regular gardener but it really does make a splendid impression on a guest's arrival when the plants and tubs outside the hotel all look well cared for and attractive.

Spoke to Charlie again about the presentation of the fresh vegetables at both lunch and dinner. He agrees with me they need to look more appetising. I just can't bear it when the chefs prepare delicious food accompanied by dull-looking vegetables. I am glad we talked because the glazed carrots with fresh coriander last night looked great. The seasons make a big difference in terms of choice. We always try to use local vegetables when in season. These may be less glamorous than products flown in from Kenya or Chile, but with a little imagination they can be just as exciting.

Details for the judges of the Meridian Business Excellence award arrive and I set off on the Red Jet to Southampton. I am one of three judges this year, along with Richard Parker, who hosted the UK Awards ceremony for the BQF in London in October, and James Braithwaite, a media executive. I think back to last year, when we were all so excited and so scared having reached the finals ourselves. I don't feel fully competent to pass judgement on the extremely fine organisations that have made it through to this year's finals. I find myself sitting there behind a big table, asking the chief executives of companies, turning over millions and employing hundreds, 'pertinent' questions. I trust my instincts and natural business acumen and get on with the judging.

The winner in the larger business category is easy, but selecting the best in the smaller business category is incredibly hard. My heart goes out to each finalist and I want them all to be winners. The televised programme isn't easy either. During my on-screen interview with Carol Vorderman, I completely forget to mention the Seaview Hotel. I just keep banging on about the Isle of Wight. My son Ben, who accompanied me to the dinner in place of Nick, says I was like a talking Island commercial. Not very sharp hotel marketing on my part. During the dinner Ben and I are fascinated to meet James Dyson, inventor of the rival to the Hoover, though he prefers not to use what he refers to as 'the H word'. He was at school with Nick and is particularly charming to Ben. He tells us all that he attributes part of his success to the fact that when he was at school he was a long-distance runner. He realised that when it really began to hurt him, it was painful for all the other runners too and if he could just put up with the pain he could win. We thought it was very true of running a small business too.

The local Education Department is holding a private dinner for thirty guests in the Sunshine Restaurant. Not naturally a front-of-house person, I always worry about functions when Nick is away. There is a lot more pressure when you need to properly orchestrate and conduct the serving of food and drink for a large party, but everything runs smoothly.

The couple in Room 2 are absolutely delighted after we upgraded them to a larger front room with a sea view, which, as it turned out, was the one their friends had raved about and specifically recommended. Another couple, who had dined at the hotel the week before and mentioned they would return for a special birthday, are thrilled with the surprise cake we have given them. Janet Saville, the talented marketing officer from Wightlink Ferry Company, comes to stay with her husband to celebrate their wedding anniversary, and they too are delighted to be upgraded. Noting and remembering all these very personal details is what sets a fine establishment above the rest. It is such a simple thing for us to do, notice a birthday or put someone in a better room if one is free, and the result is always very happy guests. It is the challenge of always being that cut above.

Saturday night and the food looks really good. We have a run on scallops for some reason. It's rather like a lottery, you just never know which items will be winners on any given night. In the summer, when every night is busy, it is easy to carry large stocks of everything, but in winter, in order to assure that everything is fresh, we reduce stock. This can result in an item running out if everyone chooses to eat the same dish. Luckily, we have enough scallops, seared with bacon and samphire, to satisfy everyone. Charlie has been so supportive during Nick's break, but the ancient mariner just called, and I am trying to kid him that a taxi is collecting him from the airport. In fact, I am driving up to meet him off the aeroplane at Gatwick. It will be so good to have him back steering the ship. I've missed him.

Mrs James has finished all the undercloths for the Sunshine tables – they look great, like full heavy blue petticoats under white ball gowns, just what the tables needed to finish off the room. I am now keen to get on with the revamp of the front restaurant. All the new fabrics have just arrived and I am testing out different shades of terracotta for the paint. Still, all that will have to wait till January. I must check on the plans for the new lighting, too. I've learnt that lighting can make or break the room. I can't tell you technically what works or doesn't in lighting. I just study the latest designs and wander round lighting departments. It used to be no overhead, only low lights, now it's all very specific lighting. But I plan and I discuss with the electricians what will work. I also need to rethink the paintings in the restaurant and replace the old watercolours originally from our dining room in London that have been in the restaurant since the beginning in 1980. At the same time I check out the order for the new air-conditioning unit.

There is concern about Amanda, a Spanish student who is working for us while learning to speak English. Her mother has been taken seriously ill. She may need to return to Spain. I find coping with staff traumas easier since taking my counselling course. But, with teenagers of my own, I always feel so sorry for young staff when they are away from home.

After a hectic day myself, I think I need counselling. Nick's first morning back and all the catching up and handing over puts us under pressure. So a brisk ride across Alan Aylett's field, known locally as 'three-quarter-mile gallop', with our dogs chasing behind, then off to the Wight Training and Enterprise Board meeting. I find the paperwork the directors are asked to read before the meeting difficult, there is just so much. I gather that the load is normal for civil servants and I can't help but wonder if it helps them justify their existence.

A woman staying with us wants to know the precise shade of green paint in the reception hall. I hate to tell her but I haven't got a clue, it was mixed up specially to match a particular colour of fabric. It is funny how people like the bold colours I use, they always remark on them. It must be about being brave, taking a risk, at least I like to think so.

It seems to have been the month for exchanging ideas. Back in the summer, Hilary Rubinstein retired from editorship of the *Good Hotel Guide*. For years he was the reigning critic of small independent hotels. The *Daily Telegraph* published an article on his favourite top ten hotels. We were lucky enough to be one of his best. Another of the hotels on his list, the Evesham, just north of the Cotswolds, has organised a special dinner for us all to come together and present Hilary with a cartoon map of the British Isles which pinpoints his ten favourite hotels. We drive up to Evesham on a Sunday afternoon in late November to be introduced to the others on Hilary's list. I was particularly interested in meeting the legendary Allen family from the Ballymaloe House in Shanagarry, near Cork in southern Ireland. We've wanted to go to stay at Ballymaloe for years, especially when the children were younger, but somehow we never managed to get the time off. They are just as I expected, a charming cosmopolitan Irish family with so many different facets and talents. I particularly like Mrs Allen, the matriarchal head of the family. She is a woman after my own heart and I am so encouraged to hear her views on using and promoting local food. She has been working on this issue with the EU and we have a great chat about my position on the Tourism Forum with Chris Smith, the Culture Secretary.

We also met Graeme Jameson, the owner of a highly successful inn near us in Winchester, the Wykeham Arms. I stayed there last January, and was especially impressed with the bedrooms, particularly in a small annexe across the road, which had exquisite attention to detail. All these successful establishments have overflows. We wanted to meet Graeme, and are delighted he is at the Evesham. He proves to be another like-minded spirit, combining a busy, sociable bar trade, good food and exceptional accommodation. The magic formula, like ours, is his staff of well-trained, charming, happy employees. Spending time with our colleagues in the trade is without question the most productive way of developing new ideas for our business.

One final meeting in November is a 'test visit' by Chris and Sue Garnett. Early last spring we went up to Scotland to a hotel conference and Chris, one of our regular customers, who is chief executive of Great North Eastern Railways (GNER), invited us to travel up on one of their trains and give our professional view of their new restaurant service. It was a fascinating trip and especially interesting to observe yet another aspect of our profession, though I think Nick really preferred standing with the driver in his cab as the train topped 100mph. to observing some poor chap trying to serve wine at that speed. After the return journey, we wrote a brief report, which we hoped would be constructive to the new catering department.

Now Chris and Sue have come down to do the same for us. They check in as normal guests and stay for the night, just like hotel inspectors. Over the years we have asked a number of relatives and friends to help us by doing test stays. Their comments are invaluable – all feedback is useful, if sometimes hard to accept. The Garnetts' suggestions are particularly helpful, especially on a fault they notice at breakfast. When they arrive at the door of the restaurant there is no one there to greet them and they are unsure where to sit. Moments later Philippa returns from the kitchen and settles them at their table. But it is those first few seconds of uncertainty when we must ensure someone is always there to greet guests. This fault has occurred before, so we feel determined to eliminate that particular problem. Meeting and greeting guests is a priority no hotel or restaurant can afford to ignore.

Chris asks Nick and me to go up to York this summer to talk to the top forty managers of GNER about winning the business award, and how we work at the Seaview. Nick and I find that exchanging ideas between very different businesses, as well as similar organisations, can be enormously beneficial to all concerned. It helps you to keep

CHAPTER 3

December
Turkey and Tinsel

I have to admit to a terrible secret. I dread Christmas. In the Crown Hotel in Ryde, where I was born, my parents used to cover the bar in cotton wool and turn it into a grotto. They were famous for their wonderful decorations and they became famous for much more. 'Take those bloody mince pies out of the oven or we will never get this baby,' the doctor shouted to my father in the middle of the Christmas Day lunch, 1953. My mother had carefully prepared the family feast and was more concerned about what she had left in the oven than about the birth of her second daughter, me. I was to be the bonus in their lunchtime Christmas cracker.

My father, Lionel Albert Bailey, married my mother, Pamela Mary Smith, in 1947. She had moved down to Bonchurch on the Isle of Wight at the end of the war when her eccentric father had decided to retire from his London business at the age of forty-five. After a long search, Grandpa Smith had found Vinnicombe, a large rambling house that could accommodate the six adolescent children plus the billiard table. They arrived complete not only with the table but also with

Grandpa's two aeroplanes, which he kept at the aerodrome in Cowes. Like so many other families at that time, torn apart by evacuation and the London bombing, their new Island home felt safe because it reunited the family in one place.

Night after night my mother went with her brothers to their local, the Freemasons' Arms in Ventnor. There the landlady would tell romantic tales of her only son, the war hero. When he finally returned, his mother had already selected Pamela from a string of girls. She was the one for 'her boy', and even before my mother set eyes on Lionel, she decided she was in love and would indeed marry him. When he appeared indifferent to this idea, my mother became obsessive. She was not used to being ignored. Finally, he mentioned in passing that after they were married they would have their own hotel. She was stunned by this news. He never proposed, he just told her that's the way it would be.

Shortly after their marriage they took over the London Hotel in Ryde. It was an insignificant establishment at the very top of the town. They were lucky to get it. After the war the breweries were inundated with requests from young couples to manage pubs and hotels all over the country. Running such a place was every returning soldier's dream. The newly married Baileys were determined to make a success of the venture. Within a short time, in spite of their customers having to climb up the hill to get a drink, they found they had the knack and had built up a roaring trade in the pub. Then the commercial travellers made their way up to the London, as bedrooms were let and things started to take off in earnest – packed bars, busy rooms and good food, the ideal formula for success.

My father was an ingenious man. He redirected the entire hotel's hot water system to run through his greenhouse, so he could provide fresh vegetables out of season, bounty in time of rationing. In no time at all, with his natural flair in the kitchen, he had built up a large following in the restaurant.

After the birth of my elder sister Anne, the brewery began to realise they were on to a winner. The Baileys had outgrown the London Hotel and needed to move on. Going up in the world meant moving halfway down the High Street to the centre of town and into the Crown Hotel. There they were able to expand their trade and develop their talents further. While my father travelled across the water to train under a Swiss chef, called Nice, at Highbury College in Portsmouth, my mother set her organisational skills and natural business acumen into motion.

The Crown was a charming small Georgian hotel with tremendous potential. Soon it was bursting at the seams. Lionel and Pamela Bailey were a great success. So after I rudely arrived in a hotel bedroom and interrupted the Christmas lunch, I was swept into the business.

It soon became apparent that the only way to the top for the Baileys was down to the seafront and a bigger challenge. They also realised that while the brewery had been good to them, they needed to go it alone if they were to achieve real success.

After the war the Isle of Wight was in a state of transition. It was still living on its faded Victorian glory, having hosted not only the entire royal family at Osborne House but also countless Victorian celebrities like Alfred Lord Tennyson, Charles Dickens and the early photographer Margaret Cameron. By the mid fifties however, things were changing. Though Ryde was a sleepy coastal town, it had one great advantage. The paddle steamer from Portsmouth docked at the end of its long pier, where steam trains and old electric trams, packed with hordes of day trippers and weekly visitors, trundled up and down between the ferry and the Esplanade.

Money was tight. Early one season a rumour spread that there was an outbreak of polio on the Island. Bookings for that summer were cancelled overnight. My parents managed to survive because they had a good local trade in both bars and the restaurant, but a good many other hotels went under. As any bank manager at the time will recall, the hotel business was an unreliable trade. Yet as hard as times were, it was a good time for the Baileys to look for a place of their own.

The Royal Esplanade Hotel was a huge Victorian establishment right on the seafront and opposite the station. It had style and elegance but was virtually bankrupt. For a £2,000 down payment and a total of £25,000, they could buy it. For them it was a fortune and a real gamble. They sold everything, including their splendid white Ford Zephyr convertible, with red flash and white-wall tyres, and moved down to the seafront.

The day they arrived they were so short of cash they didn't have enough money to stock the bar. My father made up wonderful concoctions with tea and coloured water to fill the bottles. Only the actual bottles in use on the optics contained real spirit. When they ran out they had to take money out of the till and run round to the local off-licence to get the next bottle.

The Baileys found themselves the proud owners of a seventy-eight-bedroom hotel, riddled with cockroaches and with an electrical system that was guaranteed to burn the place to the ground within a week. It had some splendid rooms overlooking the sea but others were filthy broom cupboards and none of them had a private bathroom. The task ahead was gigantic.

Slowly my father decorated, room by room, floor by floor, while at the same time dreaming of building his ideal restaurant on the roof of the hotel. There he planned to serve 'his kind of food', classical French cuisine – with no choice, but it would be the best. He imagined how diners would watch, through the restaurant's panoramic windows, the spectacular parade of ocean-going liners entering Southampton waters. Sadly it was only ever a dream – the rooftop restaurant was never built.

My sister Annie and I grew up among the staff, guests, chandeliers and saucepans. When I was three we were joined by my parents' son and heir,

William. He was known as Bumble, 'little bee', as opposed to my father, who was 'big bee'.

A hotel is a strange place to live as a child. I used to pretend I was a lift attendant and stand in the wardrobe of Room 58, open and closing the door, and announcing each floor of a department store. In Room 2 I became a Spanish princess because I knew King Alfonso of Spain had lived in the royal suite of apartments on that floor.

In an attic store, huge crown-shaped decorations that had been used for the Coronation celebrations were now stored. They were my real treasure trove. My sister and I would force off chunks of coloured glass and after hours of washing and polishing, we would entertain guests with our royal horde of rubies, emeralds and sapphires.

I also discovered that if I took my entire collection of teddies down to the front hall and arranged them on the giant chair in front of the old long-case clock, everyone would flock to admire them, before they entered the dining room. Those guests would shower me and the teddies with threepenny bits and sixpences. I saved this bounty and used it later in the forbidden world of the amusement arcade, along the seafront. It was a place my mother warned me never to enter, so naturally I went there to ride on Muffin the mechanical Mule or, worse still, play bingo. I'm not sure which was more exciting, the arcade rides and games or the fear of being caught in a forbidden place, full of boys with Brylcreemed hair, drainpipe jeans and tattooed limbs.

In the corner of the hotel ballroom was a grey monstrosity which, when turned on, would slowly light up and glow. It played 78rpm records and had a radio. My treat was to put on Danny Kaye singing 'The Ugly Duckling', and dance around alone on the highly polished ballroom floor.

My godmother Julia Roberts was a receptionist at the Royal Esplanade Hotel. She was also in love with my favourite Uncle Jim, my mother's youngest brother and the hotel manager. I loved them both dearly. In her spare time I would go up to her room at the top of the hotel where she would recount Rudyard Kipling's *Just So Stories*. She had huge brown eyes with long sweeping black lashes, which she would roll as she told the tale of the Elephant Child and the Great Grey-green Greasy Limpopo river. On her day off, she and Uncle Jim would take me over to Ventnor on the southernmost tip of the Island, in his gleaming red car with a special seat for me in the boot. We would race over the downs, dropping down the steep hills to the coast, and there I would spend the day with Julia's family. Her beautiful niece Kim, a gentle child, had nearly died at birth of a hole in the heart and was now dying of leukaemia. I was terrified watching young beauty decaying before my eyes and hearing everyone saying she was going to die. Lunch at the Roberts' was baked beans on toast, something I never had in the hotel. On the way home we would drive past the gates of the house of one of the Island's most famous ghosts, the 'headless horseman', and Julia would recount the tale of how at night he would ride over the downs looking for his lost love, his head hacked off by her wicked father. I would always get collywobbles in my tummy as she told the story.

In the Royal Esplanade we took our meals on the family table, with its crisp white linen tablecloth. I longed to have tea in a proper home instead of dinner in a hotel restaurant, where we were served by a string of foreign waiters. They all had a wiggle in their walk and could carry rows of plates that stretched the full length of their arms. One in particular, called Danny, would admire himself in the mirror while polishing glasses, turning from left to right and back again, checking out his best side. They all called me 'Miss Nicky'.

My father worked mainly in the kitchens, which were below ground level. They were thrilling. A labyrinth of stores, fridges and cupboards, filled with a constant air of excitement bordering on chaos. My father was a huge man with masses of hair, bushy eyebrows and a gentle aura. Everything seemed in control when he was around and I felt safe. Situated in the centre of the main kitchen was the range. He would glide around it in a magical way, working on a dozen things at once. From one end excited waiters would rush in demanding this or that 'away' and while they muttered some foreign obscenity, he would keep them waiting. If he were baking, I would use up his scraps of pastry, moulding each piece like putty in my small unwashed hands, sometimes dropping lumps on the floor. Picking them up I would squeeze and shape pastry biscuits. When they were like speckled grey rubber I would ask him to cook them for me in his big ovens. My unfortunate victims were the receptionists, whom I would invite to sample my charming titbits and who were unable to refuse as my father towered over them, laughing. They must have been disgusting.

For a child, the kitchen was a secret kingdom under the hotel, filled with huge, complicated equipment and wonderful smells. I loved to watch the enormous mixer churn round or the mincer spew out its mottled products. There were times when the kitchen was packed with steaming men and filled with the din of clattering plates and pans. At other times of the day it was empty and dark, with just the gentle roll of the stockpot brewing. Either way, it was magic to me.

Sometimes, depending on the moon, a high spring tide and torrential rain, the whole labyrinth would flood. Incredibly, nothing stopped. Men worked in wellingtons and I stood forlorn like Paddington Bear as water lapped over the top of my small boots. Like a theatrical performance, nothing ever interrupted the hotel service. Once, when my mother fainted during a busy function, she was left gently alone. The show must go on.

I became my father's shadow. I watched. I listened. Early each morning, he took his clipboard of orders to the switchboard. There he would stand and phone each supplier. He knew how to get the best out of people and they loved giving it to him. He stuttered – a legacy from a hard war. I stuttered.

He felt passionately about food – I felt passionately about food. When he went on his weekly trip around the suppliers I went too. We would walk into the various shops – Pink's the grocers and victuallers of the Royal Yacht, Arnold's the greengrocer, Harry Ross the butcher with his young son Colin, Tim's the fishmongers and Barnet's the poultry specialist. My father was a fiercely loyal man and the suppliers who had helped him when he started at the London Hotel were key players now. He would stand discussing the season while critically testing supplies, and included me as his prize taster. My views were not always what Mr Arnold wanted to hear about his prize fruit. At Pink's, the aroma of fresh ground coffee beans and ripening cheese greeted you, as there was no compulsion to refrigerate then. I felt very small below the towering shelves packed with exotic jars and tins. Food was still short and some rationing still applied. My father commanded immense respect, always managed to obtain what he needed and would wink at me as we walked out laden with delicious ingredients for the menu.

To watch the orchestration of service was fascinating. A finishing touch to this dish or a sprig of parsley on that plate. Father had a critical eye and an inexhaustible capacity for work. Eventually the kitchen moved up to ground level, solving the wellington problem and also supplying me with a tiny round wooden flap seat where I settled back during service and watched the bustle and soaked in the smells.

Some afternoons I would rush home from school to find a particular culinary surprise. Once it was a perfectly moulded model of the Island sculpted in spinach; on another occasion a flight of choux-pastry swans. Father would stop to explain what he had done and how he had achieved it.

Later, towards the end of his shortened life, he would always be ill at Christmas, and we often spent the holiday with him in the coronary care unit at St Mary's Hospital, in Newport, looking out over Parkhurst Prison. I grew to dislike hospitals as much as I disliked Christmas. I loathed all the hospital equipment and the gathering smell of slow, tragic death would frighten me for years afterwards. My father managed to survive until shortly after my twenty-first birthday, when he gave me a wonderful party at the Berkeley Hotel in London. My parents were staying in a beautiful suite in the Athenaeum Hotel on Piccadilly, where Nick Hayward was then a young junior manager. But we didn't know him then. I had always thought that my father, with all his war stories and songs, was invincible, but now he was a crumpled old man of fifty-five with a fatal heart condition. He died on 1st March 1975, and I wanted to die too. At Christmas, instead of happily celebrating my birthday I encounter the ghosts of Christmas past.

Now at the Seaview we try to get the decorations up by 1st December in readiness for the numerous Christmas parties which start from the beginning of the month. The public bar is draped in masses of tinsel and fairy lights until, with its open fire, it is brimming with a festive pantomime-like atmosphere. The decorations go up all over the ground floor. Individual Christmas trees are placed on each of the restaurant tables. I have some beautiful decorations for the front restaurant, which are individually hand-painted gold and silver shells done by Sheila Holmes, a local lady. I hang them on the window so they can be seen when people pass the restaurant as they walk down to the main reception desk and I feel pleased with my efforts. The rest of the hotel is, we hope, rather more subtle, dignified and delicate than the public bar.

For the last two years, we have closed for four days over Christmas. It was a difficult financial decision to close. But so many of our loyal and long-standing staff had worked continuously over both Christmas and the New Year and deserved a break. We had a series of discussions during our weekly meetings and finally put it to the vote. We knew that to close at Christmas would result in a loss of revenue at a crucial time of year, but this was weighed up against the immense enjoyment it would give our employees and their families to be able to enjoy the celebrations together, at home. Everyone agreed that we would look at the loss and that this would be reflected in the salary increases in May. When you involve the people who work in a business in its running decisions you discover how sensibly they act concerning its destiny. One of the BQF assessors told me that a member of our team had said, 'The Seaview Hotel is not just Nick and

Nicky's business, it's our livelihood too.' Obviously the Christmas closure results in a loss of revenue and custom, but not as much as we feared.

Over the years we have received very few complaints in the restaurant, but one particularly difficult lady felt that our Christmas Day special lunch at £24 per person for five courses was too expensive. Trying to look constructively at the criticism in this lady's complaint, we all felt despondent. We had purposely kept the price as inexpensive as possible. Her menu included Scotch smoked salmon rolls filled with fresh local crab meat, home-made game soup, fresh local roast turkey with all the trimmings, Christmas pudding and brandy butter with home-made mince pies and cream, followed by coffee and local mints. The cost of the wages alone, at double time, made it hard to cover the cost of the food. And with the five rich courses, using top-quality expensive ingredients, we found it hard to justify the complaint. So when we decided to stop the lunch altogether it was not only better for our loyal employees but also avoided any criticism of the price. Some people find it hard to understand and allow for the extra wage costs. Anyway, it is my birthday.

We do a special dinner in both our bars on a quiet night early in December, especially popular with the locals. There's roast turkey with all the trimmings, Brussels sprouts and carrots, crackers and mince pies, all for £6.50 a head. It makes a lovely evening around the fire in the public bar, all the tables laid with white linen cloths and the whole place looking really smart. It enables as many people as possible to enjoy Seaview during the festive season. We have not altered the price in three years, as it is our way of thanking all the local people for their support.

One problem at this time of year is too much festive spirit, as landlords and taxi drivers know only too well. I fear the drunkenness, the forced gaiety and the occasional abuse. Early in the month the first of the parties start. Set menus, crackers, pretty dresses. The older chefs concentrate on the turkey, sprouts and roast potatoes, while the younger lads hang out of the kitchen door eyeing up the pretty girls on their way to the loos. Paper hats and giggles all round. Tempo begins to build.

Our first Christmas at the Seaview was no giggle. I was pregnant with Pip and Ben was just two. We worked so hard and were so exhausted at the end of a long day on Christmas Eve that we almost missed Father Christmas. Then on New Year's Eve we had a fancy dress party. There aren't many things you can go as when you are eight and a half months pregnant so I dressed up as a bumblebee. I even had smart antennae made out of wire coat hangers and topped with ping-pong balls. As mid-night approached it looked as though two local lads were about to start a fight. Nick had just disappeared into the restaurant and I was left to deal with the lads by the front door. Just as I started to sternly tick them off, one of my antennae collapsed, they immediately stopped arguing and burst out laughing. I got the job as bouncer from then on. I also had the job of chief cook and bottle washer.

So after my childhood down in the kitchens of the Royal Esplanade, the tiny kitchen at the Seaview easily became a natural habitat. My father had given me no formal cookery lessons but he had taught me how to make all the classic sauces. Since then, using a copy of *Mastering the Art of French Cookery* and Katie Stewart's instruction manual, I had grown to simply love to cook. I was, however, not prepared for all the cooking I had to do when we came to the Seaview. I learnt fast and would stand surrounded by my copper pots and pans, imagining that I was liaising with my father again. If that was just a dream, the first Christmas was quite a shock. All work and cooking and no time with our small son. Later, when I pulled back from the kitchen, I looked back on those early years with considerable horror. I just don't know how I worked so hard, with our young family.

By mid December the Christmas party season is into a real swing. One night we have three parties taking place in three separate areas of the hotel. In the Sunshine Restaurant a rather professional festive dinner is held by some Island accountants and solicitors, while in the front bar a private Christmas meal is held for the local health authority. The loud male voices raised in song come from the remnants of the local builders' and electricians' lunchtime turkey dinner. They are slowing down now, almost speechless but periodically raising their voices to confirm they are still here.

Meanwhile the chairman of the Isle of Wight Council is entertaining the High Sheriff of the Island in the more sedate front restaurant, but they are not happy, as the Sheriff's wife and the chairman want to smoke. Luckily during the evening they manage to gatecrash one or two of the other parties for a fag break.

At the same time as serving people in funny paper hats, we have been planning the work that will begin immediately after our return from holiday in the New Year. So as we guide the builders off the premises following their Christmas party, we hope they will sober up in time to start the hotel refurbishing. This year, once again, the party season passes off without incident. All parties are over and we shut up the hotel on the night of Wednesday 23rd December with our own party. I warn our staff not to leave any unpleasant deposits as a result of over-indulgence, as they all know how ghastly it is having to clear up. Over the years our staff parties have toned down as we have got older. I dare not look at some of the photographs of me in the early days. Now we have two parties a year. The first is at the end of the summer season. By September the team are exhausted but united. During the peak month of August the adrenaline really flows every night. So before we say goodbye to the summer students returning to college, and to thank everyone for yet another season, we arrange a dinner and disco on a Sunday night early in September, in a private room at the Old Fort pub just down the road on the seafront. This party tends to be most popular with the younger staff and Nick and I worried as more and more of our long-standing older employees dropped out. Especially the parents, who felt they had to be responsible for the younger ones and found they could not really enjoy themselves. So we all decided that the full-time staff would come out for a Christmas dinner the first night that the hotel is closed. This year it has been arranged by Bob the chef and Fay the head housekeeper and is to be at a small Italian restaurant at the top of Ryde, called Salvatores.

The party starts with drinks in the front bar and a Christmas raffle at which everyone gets a prize. Then Nick and I and the children distribute presents to everyone and Nick makes a small speech. This year we are all thrilled by winning the award, and Nick makes a point that it is their dedication and commitment which has enabled the Seaview to succeed. It is a jolly party and I feel so proud when I look round the room at the happy faces who are the power behind the Seaview. The dinner in Ryde is clearly a success as merry members of the team wobble out, to where I am waiting stone-cold sober and ready to ferry them on to the next stage. Suddenly the car is full, including the boot, with hotel chefs, and Pip and Jules are squashed in next to their intoxicated father. We drive off to the Balcony Bar, a disco on Ryde seafront, where I am very concerned that there may be a limit to how many chefs you are allowed in a VW Golf. When we arrive, Nick explains that his men need him and he has to stay. Ben also remains

CHAPTER 4

January
Weddings and Funerals

Our annual family skiing holiday is one of our few getaways of the year. On 27th December, while the hotel is still shut for Christmas, we fly to Val d'Isère. It's a precious week on our calendar. The same evening we are featured on Isle of Wight Radio, a kind of Desert Island Discs. Local broadcaster John Hannam came to the hotel just before Christmas and recorded a programme in which Nick and I talked about our recent success and looked back on our history at the hotel. We also chose some songs with a vaguely culinary connection (the Ink Spots and Java Jive's 'I like coffee, I like tea' and Ella Fitzgerald's 'Mack the Knife') and a song picked by our children, who for years have endured our obsessive need to ensure that our hotel always remains impeccable: 'It's got to be perfect' by Fairground Attraction.

Ben, Pip and Jules are all with us as we set off from Gatwick to Lyon. I am aware that this may be our last family holiday together. Ben, at nearly twenty-one, is a man now. Next winter we expect Pip will be away on her gap year between school and university. Jules, at fifteen, will soon be the only one at home. On the holiday we are accompanied by my brother, William, and his son Gregory.

The idea is to share a family chalet for a week of relaxation and skiing. The reality, however, especially with my brother William being a fellow hotelier, is much time spent discussing work. Our young know how to switch off. They understand how hard we find it to let go of our profession, even for this week. Like the Seaview, the Royal Hotel at Ventnor was in a very run-down state when William bought it four years ago, and he has since completely turned the business around. This year the Royal has just been upgraded by the English Tourist Board to become the first four-star hotel on the Isle of Wight. With over fifty bedrooms, a huge restaurant, conference room, bar, swimming pool and extensive grounds, it is a big operation. We work closely together. William has great marketing skills while Nick and I have years of experience on what works on the Island.

Some sibling rivalry erupts: both William and I have recently acquired new laptop computers. William has the superior model, complete with a modem link into the computerised booking system at the Royal. Mine is modemless. While driving up the steep mountain pass to Val d'Isère, at the touch of a finger William can scan the occupancy figures in Ventnor. The new technology is amazing but does not let you relax. It allows you to have a constant peek at the business. We arrive at the chalet and unpack, but I soon telephone Seaview to find out how things are and to hear how the radio interview sounded. Apparently it was great, according to my mum at least.

While our athletic youngest daughter Jules and her cousin Gregory ski down the steepest black run before breakfast, I come to terms with the fact that my skiing technique gets worse as I get older. I can't be bothered with the steep and icy stuff, so I give up and stick to the easy runs. Nick, who stopped competing with our son's more aggressive skiing when Ben was fourteen, is keen to show William, five years his junior, just how fit he is. Everyone begins to relax, calm down and ski more. Each evening I ring the hotel to get a progress report on what's happened and what lies ahead. I talk to most of the key staff and get a picture of exactly how the hotel is doing, while we're away. (As you can see, we are never really away). I am told very firmly by Leon that the only problem at the Seaview is my interfering phone calls. I know I need to leave the team at the hotel to get on with their job and stop constantly nagging but I find it so hard to delegate and let go. William, meanwhile, is linked directly to his system and can check for himself without making nuisance calls.

When I am not phoning home or sliding down the mountain dressed like Scott of the Antarctic or moving about like Mr Blobby, Nick and I are analysing and guessing how much the mountain resort restaurants take in a season. After years in catering we know exactly how they order, store and prepare the food halfway up a snow-covered mountain for the vast numbers of skiers they feed every day at lunchtime. We can immediately spot the efficient operations and also note one of the worst mountain cafes we have ever encountered. It is brand new this season and they are clearly very inexperienced. Appalled at the level of incompetence, we compare it to the height of the summer season at Seaview when orders for food in the bars flood in and we can easily become swamped. We can't turn people away because, unlike in our restaurant, you don't book tables, you simply turn up and order. All we can do when we are very busy is warn people that there will be a delay. It usually does the trick. Even on the most crowded nights in August it is not more than about half an hour. We have just wasted an hour and a half waiting for a disgusting lunch. It reminds us that when we are packed to the rafters at the Seaview, we must get it right so customers will return despite a wait. We all decide never to come to this particular mountain cafe again.

The week flies by and in no time William and I are tapping away at our respective laptops as we travel round the hairpin bends back down the mountain towards Lyon. I have to confess that while he is locked into the Royal's occupancy I am playing solitaire. Judging by the bleary state of the older children's eyes they clearly had a good time in Dick's famous tea-bar last night.

*

Willie Caws and Rob Hermans head the local firm of builders – 'firm' being the operative word. They virtually run Seaview and Willie's ancestors built and owned much of the centre of the village back in the early 1800s. When we first bought the hotel they came in and 'got us sorted'. In nearly two decades they have meticulously transformed the hotel, by both filling our tills and emptying our bank account. Nothing they do is ever cheap, but everything is of a very high standard. They worked with us, never for us.

Our first day back in January and the hotel winter redecoration starts. Now we are greeted by the entire crew of builders and electricians, stripping out the front restaurant for a complete revamp before the Millennium.

Why do workmen always make so much noise and mess? Do they always need to play radios? They have no idea of demarcation, no sense of where outdoor stops and indoor begins, and somehow they reduce everything to an open-air building site. What's more, the fact that the money to pay them comes from serving our guests seems to escape their notice. The early stages of any refurbishment seems to result in much mess and noise, accompanied by a need for endless supplies of hot drinks. Since we are open for business as usual, the atmosphere is tense. If only we could hide them away out of sight and sound of the guests!

When we first arrived at the Seaview things were similarly fraught. My mother and her team of workmen and decorators from the Royal Esplanade Hotel, along with my multi-talented Uncle Jim, all rallied round. I had not wanted my family to guarantee the bank loan, though Dickie Brice, our original bank manager, would have been far happier if they had. My parents banked with Barclays. We did the same, but while we had an excellent relationship with the bank from the start, Nick and I needed to buy the Seaview on our own. But I was most grateful to my mother for the loan of her skilled craftsmen to help our initial refurbishment.

Cecil the painter and decorator arrived and transformed the original red-and-gold flock wallpaper in the restaurant and front bar, using a fashionable jade green paint we had used in our dining room in Clapham. Uncle Jim fixed all the creaking floorboards, hung pictures and clocks, hammered and sawed, screwed up and cut down until the place looked reasonably presentable. He was so good to us in the early years, and has always been like a second father to me, even giving me away at my wedding. He never married my godmother Julia, who left the Island when I was thirteen to live in California. Years later, when we all thought Jim was a confirmed bachelor, he married Shirley, a wonderful, bubbly character who supported him and us from the very start. We would have been lost without them, always ready to lend a hand, helping behind the bar, even running the whole business when Nick and I desperately needed a break.

Lionel Cook, my mother's carpet and upholstery supplier, concealed all the worn-out threadbare pieces of carpet on the steps of the front staircase, moving everything up six inches, so that the worn pieces were on the riser and less easily noticed. He then coloured in the bare patches with felt-tip pen. It was two years before we had to replace the carpet. Brian, the carpenter, fitted a solid wooden top to the public bar. Dottie, the head receptionist for years at Ryde, walked into Seaview along the sea wall to help run the hotel office, and the old restaurant manager Pedro came in to help carry plates. Then Chef, from the Esplanade (to this day I still think of him as Chef or Cheffy), gave me one of his old knives, which had once belonged to my father. I stood in the kitchen and treasured its every action.

Now, we know in our hearts that Caws & Hermans the builders are real craftsmen, and that the work they do will be of the highest possible standard when complete. Just as in those early days when we took over and had to blitz the place, refurbishment has to be done each year, and though you know it will be better afterwards, during the process it's painful.

With the front restaurant out of commission for weeks, we start to think of ideas for the new spring menu. The restaurant menu is changed every six to eight weeks, and the whole bar and restaurant menu changed four times a year. A brainstorming menu-planning session with the chefs takes place around the table on a quiet January morning. Everyone from the kitchen is there, from Charlie, head chef and old-timer, to Nigel, a fairly new wash-up recruit. We cook up ideas and talk food. Recipe books are scattered over the table, including one by my current favourite, Nigel Slater's *Real Food* – so naughty and indulgent. Here is a man after my own heart, though not good for the diet. No swopping of clotted cream for crème fraîche, or avoiding the rich, full ripe, melted Camembert for Mr Slater. We discuss the pros and cons of each dish and analyse how difficult they will be to produce when we are really busy. Having steamed away like a galley slave in our tiny kitchen myself, I am genuinely aware of exactly what can and cannot be produced at the Seaview at different times of year. In the winter we simply avoid dishes that require large stocks of expensive perishable ingredients and can result in costly wastage, but in summer we have to be very careful. Too many grilled large flat fish like plaice, lemon or Dover sole, can block up the salamander grills, and with only six burners and a solid-top range we are limited on the number of items we can cook on the top at any one time. Then there is the fryer – too many chips or deep-fried fish must be avoided.

I love these sessions. It is such a good way for members of the team to discover their strengths and show ingenuity. With everyone's contribution we always arrive at a consensus and develop some great ideas. A starter of smoked fish and horseradish mash with hot grilled pesto bread. Honey-roast best end of lamb with coriander carrot and deep-fried aubergine. Roasted cod with tomato basil and olive crust on pea purée and seared tuna with garlic potato crush and onion rings, followed by rich winter desserts like spiced rice pudding with warm winter berries. Charlie and Bob, his 'second', had some ambitious and delicious ideas but I was worried about the amount of pastry work and preparation needed in the cold area which would put pressure, before and during service, on the new and younger members of the team. We make our final decisions and the boys agree to try their dishes on a busy night as a trial run. Trial and error is not only the best test but also enables the chefs to learn as they experiment. I suggest a return to some classic and uncomplicated ideas which are much loved by Seaview regulars, like crab cakes and poached meringues known as floating islands. The chefs look bored. We compromise, we admire the cookbook pictures, we dream up more dishes, everyone's taste taking us in wonderful directions.

When I first started as the naive chef at the Seaview, back in 1980, I brought with me my childhood experiences combined with a female instinct for housekeeping. I always loved sitting up in bed at night browsing through cookery books, Katie Stewart and Mrs Beeton, Paul Bocuse and Anton Mosimann and of course the then-young Delia. Having eaten in my parents' hotel dining room from an early age, I feel totally at home in hotel restaurants and the kitchen. I was thrilled to discover recently that Nick and I, and any of our employees, could go out to lunch or dinner in a restaurant and that the experience could legitimately be called 'benchmarking' and referred to as 'work'. Though we try to go to as many new restaurants as possible, in reality it is hard for us to leave the Seaview so time prohibits us abusing this particular work experience.

At the beginning, I thought of the restaurant as a large dinner party of friends. The only drawback was that the guests wanted a selection of different choices for each course and didn't decide which one they would eat until the last moment. But the bonus was that in return they paid us money. At Corney & Barrow there was a special dining room used to give private lunches to clients, accompanied by superb wines. The cook was a lady called Gerti. To accompany the finest Bâtard-Montrachet or Corton-Charlemagne she made the most delicious light and fluffy fish mousses. Her smoked haddock and egg would accompany whites with a more robust heritage, while her delicate crab claw mousse was perfect for the finest white Burgundy. Before I left, I learnt how to make them all from Gerti and they were an early hit at Seaview. I began to pick up trade skills, how to turn vegetables and produce works of art from a radish. Then I began to expand my repertoire, how to prepare so much more before service so it was not all a last-minute rush. I grew in confidence and became more pro-fessional. Early in 1980, once we had decided to move but before we left London, I went to train in several commercial kitchens in order to get more experience, knowing I would have to do some cooking, at least at the beginning. I had lectured to the diploma students at the Cordon Bleu School, both in Marylebone and Winkfield, for several years, but that was on wine with food, not cooking.

John Armit, managing director of Corney & Barrow, had just opened Zanzibar in Great Queen Street in Covent Garden. Part of my job was to look after the wine sales for this account. It was run by Nick Smallwood and Simon Slater, with Alastair Little as the chef. Alastair was brilliant and also generous, giving me many useful tips. It was he who insisted I purchase an industrial version of the latest must-have gadget, the Magimix, and warned me to buy two bowls so that when I had used one I wouldn't need to rush off and wash it up before doing the next bit. It has been interesting to watch the trajectory of these careers since. Alastair is now a famous restaurateur, author and TV chef, even seen on *Ready Steady Cook*, while Nick and Simon have become one of London's most successful restaurant partnerships at Launceston Place and Kensington Place, until they recently sold out to Chris Bodker. Then there was Albert Albertini, the old restaurant manager at the Athenaeum who went on to run L'Ecu de France. He allowed me to descend into his cellars at Jermyn Street to work in the huge kitchens of this classic institution, sadly no longer in existence today. Derek, the head chef of the Athenaeum, allowed me to work with him, as did Michel Bourdin of the famous Connaught Hotel. Michel, a master chef for over three decades, came down and stayed with us at the Seaview and has been a constant support since we opened. Time spent in his kitchen was an education in itself. The quality of the equipment and the enormous capital investment was staggering. The expertise of each

Connaught chef was inspirational, they were all so clever. The feeling of pride and excitement – everyone in that kitchen was aware they were at the Connaught. The housewife in me was appalled at the wastage. They made fresh ice cream every day.

One difficulty at the Seaview is that we run a smart restaurant menu in parallel with a simple village pub menu. It means you need to have a dual food personality if you want to remain sane in the kitchen. Trying to produce intricate and innovative dishes as near to *haute cuisine* as possible, and at the same time churning out vast quantities of sausage and chips, is never easy. When I was cooking, my hair and clothes became impregnated with the smell of the fryer. In the early days I made a radical decision to take all the fried food off the menu. Much healthier, I thought, better for the customers and better for me. Every day Nick would come into the kitchen with food orders begging me to change my mind, as some poor customer just wanted a few simple chips. Try as I might I just couldn't ban the fryer. The mashes and pulses so popular today just weren't fashionable food in the early eighties and we were, after all, the village pub. What do people expect in their local? Good grub, often fried, good beer and no foody pretension. For the sake of the business I returned to smelling like a chippy. I thought, if customers want it fried I'll fry. The most popular dish became fresh field mushroom dipped in thick batter and deep-fried, served with a simple crisp salad and my home-made garlic mayonnaise.

Now, with the new menus selected, we begin to

cook and try the dishes. Sometimes we all try something, sitting round a single plate with a forest of forks each taking a bit. It is rather like the tasting room at Corney & Barrow, but we don't write down our tasting notes. Other times Nick and I will try a dish for supper and then go back to the chefs in the kitchen with our views. Finally, when we are nearly ready, we put the dish on as a special and see what the customers think. After service or the next day we ask David and Leon if the guests made any comments. I am always very upfront with the customers. I tell them it is a new dish and specifically ask them if they think we should add it to the menu. Somehow the customers seem to really enjoy being part of the selection process. Some ideas work and others don't, not because they don't taste good, but often because they are tricky to prepare and serve under pressure. Or they don't look good because they are stacked up and fall over when the waiting staff are trying to carry them into the restaurant. This new menu food is tasting good – especially the spiced rice pudding – shame about my diet! All in the service of the hotel, I say, as I begin to expand.

Not only have tastes and demand for fine food developed over recent years, but the language we use to describe each dish and the way we present food on a plate have changed. What is placed before you in most modern restaurants is a work of art. Even the plates the food is served on have changed. At Le Caprice the iced berries coated in white chocolate look even better because they are served on a rich-royal-blue glass plate. Now we need to decide: do we stack or spread out the food? Do we use a small white, a large black or even our own blue glass plates? Do we dust with icing sugar or cocoa powder or do we dribble with mango juice or drizzle with walnut oil? It's a long way from the old days of simple dressed crab in its shell with a bit of fresh parsley and a wedge of lemon. I think long and hard about which words we will use on the menu, the drizzle or the dribble, to describe each dish. Then the menus have to be typed up and checked by both Charlie and me. My spelling is simply dreadful. Before the days when every small business had a photocopier I would write out each menu by hand in italics. It took at least half an hour just for a few copies and even longer when we were busy and needed more. They looked great but hardly one line was without a mistake. Now, with computer spell-checks and italic fonts on laser printers, life is much more efficient, and there are lots of people who know my failing and will point out my errors before they affront the eyes of the customers. Once the menus are drafted they will be typed up by Angela in the office, printed off and secured in the smart plain navy restaurant covers. *Voilà!*

The winter building work is running late. I changed the original specification, in order to make more room in the kitchen. Every year during the refurbishment I always think of new ideas as the work is being carried out and change the plan as we go along. It's a bit like the way I cook. I never follow a recipe properly, I know what ingredients I want to use and roughly where I want to go in terms of the finished dish, but if a better idea comes along which will improve the taste or the way the food looks, I go for it. For the builders my decorating improvisations are a nightmare. I might complain about their noise, dust and constant thirst for tea and coffee but they must get so frustrated by my continual change of programme. Because I have moved the position of the restaurant door into the kitchen, now I need to move a ceiling light. They have all collaborated with me for so long that they seem to know and understand what I'm up to even before I change it.

This is the first time any major alterations have been made to the front restaurant since the installation of the new kitchen in 1996. We are all developing a new look for the hotel and they feel the same sense of ownership of the Seaview as everyone else who works here. Nevertheless, it doesn't help that we are now running a week behind. Nor does it help that Leon, the hotel's manager, has accidentally walked across the kitchen floor tiles the builders have just laid. The tracks of my tears! Now the builders will be even more delayed as they sort out the damage. This means Mike Orchard the painter will be late, and that will in turn hold up John Betchley, the carpet fitter. He will then delay Mrs James who is to fit the upholstery and curtains, so we won't be ready to hang the new paintings before the official opening. The domino effect runs on. I try to remain positive.

Terracotta and a rich peacock blue are the new colours, with grey-tinted mirrors. The paintwork is simple white and there is a new dark wooden dado rail. At the far end of the restaurant there is an area known as a station, where all the necessities of service – wine, plates, glasses, tablecloths, napkins – are stored in a small wooden dresser. We have bought new tables, slightly larger to give the customers more room. We not only looked through many catalogues but also attended trade fairs and consulted with other friends in the industry before finally ordering the new tables. It all matches the vision I had and I am pleased. It seems such a long time since I chose the material and colours last autumn. I had a vision then, have added to my improvisation since, and now everything has fallen into place perfectly. Well, 'fallen' is not the word I should have used. Unfortunately the large mirror broke as it was being fixed to the wall. It didn't help that the manufacturers failed to drill two crucial anchoring holes on one side of the mirror. But it has been temporarily fixed and the glazier will return next week to replace it. He must feel unlucky coming to the Seaview Hotel – he broke mirrors on his last four visits and has to think that the place is jinxed or that he's in the wrong job. How unlucky can you get? In the end, despite all the building problems and delays, the opening is only two days behind. The week before, Mike Orchard worked over the weekend and late each evening to finish on time for the wedding reception lunch on Friday. It pays to use people you know. We are hanging the last pictures and Mike is touching up the paint in a corner of the mirror just as the white wedding limousine draws up outside.

The windswept bride and groom swirl into the hotel on a blustery cold January morning. I pick up the last of the dustsheets and whisk them out of sight. Picture hooks and hammer are scooped up and I rush down the corridor to the office. That really was a close one. Nick, poised as usual, is there welcoming the wedding party with his lovely grin. I sneak back into the restaurant via the kitchen to ensure everything is in place.

John Betchley, the carpet man, has done his stuff, cheerfully screeding floors and laying thick blue carpet. He had to change his entire week's schedule so the carpet would be there in good time for the wedding. A blessing, is our John.

We turned to John when Lionel Cook retired after our first frugal years covering cracks in the lino and bare patches in the carpets. Now we have enough money to buy practical, very hard-wearing contract carpets that look good but will withstand commercial wear and tear. This time we continue through into the dining room with the dark blue contract carpet we used in both the bar and Sunshine Restaurant. It looks very smart, but at over £1,200 for a fairly small area we hope it will last a few seasons to come. When we first started using John we were only able to buy the cheapest carpet. You get what you pay for and it never lasted very long. We soon learnt that it was a false economy and that if we invested in proper, thickly woven trade carpets they would withstand commercial use far better than cheap domestic ones.

On the south wall, as you walk into the restaurant, is a new addition, a set of three original paintings by Cavendish Morton. He did them in Portsmouth dockyards during the war and the strange details of working naval ships fit perfectly into the nautical ambience of the Seaview. We bought these paintings six months ago in a gallery in Bembridge. We have also collected numerous ship's dials, clocks and barometers, along with a solid brass propeller and a heavy piece of steering equipment. Now all polished and mounted by Gordon Pavey, a former schoolteacher but now artisan, on beautifully varnished hardwood, they look splendid. The room glows and has a first-class feel. The crowning glory is my new lighthouse. I spotted it in the General Trading Company in London at the end of last summer. It's French, painted terracotta and cream, ideally matching the colour of the restaurant walls, and has a light glowing inside. Just the thing for a seaside restaurant and, as we find on winter nights, a welcome homing device.

Locals arrive and staff come in to inspect our latest creation. Unfortunately, there has been a hiccup with the new menus and they have not been typed up yet. Three of the receptionists and David from the restaurant have all been down with flu and we are short-staffed. The hotel can normally run on a lower staff ratio in the winter and during this period most of the permanent staff take their holidays as well as attending training courses. This January they are tending to illness. We can still operate normally with the odd day's sickness but a flu epidemic causes major problems and disruptions. Somehow we make do and hope the guests don't notice that Philippa, who brought their breakfast, is still around turning down their beds at night. I wonder what it says in the new working time directive about flu epidemics and small companies' inability to supply a normal service to their guests when they are so short-staffed. Should we ask our employees to work longer hours to cover for the sick or do we let our customers down? We juggle and Nick and I do more. As soon as we are back to full strength and Angela returns to the office, she will finally be able to start to print the copies of the menu. It is a long job and will take her nearly all day.

Halfway through the wedding feast Seaview is plunged into darkness as the electricity goes off. It's not just the hotel – the whole village and surrounding area has suffered a blackout. No calls can get through to the hotel switchboard. None of the electronic bar tills operate as the electric drawers won't open. I suddenly wonder about my idea of painting the front restaurant ceilings dark blue. It feels gloomy in the new dining room with no lights. I light more candles and put them on the tables but the wedding party seems unperturbed.

In the public bar members of a local family are gathering before a funeral that afternoon. Arthur Birchenough, much loved-husband, father and grandfather, has passed away. In Seaview during his retirement he spread his great charm and sailing knowledge by giving lessons in his small dinghy. He also gave thousands in the village sheer delight by organising the most wonderful firework displays each August at the end of village regatta week. Somberly dressed generations of the family are lit by the warm glow of the fire. The five or six small grandchildren, distracted by the excitement of the power cut, appear to be imagining the ghost of their grandpa in the spooky light. It is a sad moment in the history of the old public bar, counterpointed by the laughter and celebration drifting across from the new restaurant.

Sir Norman Fowler, the former government minister and a regular customer, oblivious to the drama caused by the blackout, sits in the waning daylight of the hotel porch collecting his messages on his mobile, and sipping tea. Armed with portable battery-operated camping lights, I rush round to each department turning them on trying to restore some light. The boys in the kitchen are used to the drill, and at least we cook by gas. In less than an hour, power is returned and the funeral party go up the road to the local church. Sir Norman attends to his important messages and I sneak off home. I need a break. My head is buzzing with restaurant chair covers and new power-cut procedures. The proximity of revellers and mourners, and having to change faces to suit each party of guests, has stretched me.

To counter the stress, I decide to go out for a ride. We have two horses: Abby, a seventeen-hand gentle black mare, and Sir Wotabout, a seventeen-hand young gelding, normally ridden by Nick or Jules. Some people have therapy, some drink or take drugs, I ride at a good clip over the downs or along the beach away from the pressure and hubbub of hotel and Seaview. As I drive into the stable yard I'm met by Simon Reed, who owns and runs the stables. Simon helped me buy my first horse, Thomas, a Welsh cob, years ago and is my equine guru. Over the years he and his team have taught the three children to ride, taking us out together for gallops along the beach. He found the perfect pony, a tiny Welsh section A, for Jules's seventh birthday present. The funny white fluffy beast was covered in tinsel when we arrived, excited, before breakfast. Then he found Herbie, a pretty, dappled grey jumping pony for Pip to take off to Pony Club camp. Later Simon, an expert rider himself, not only encouraged Nick, at over forty, to join us and learn to ride, but then coached him to develop into the bold and brave rider he is today. Jeanette our groom has brushed and polished, trained and exercised the horses so they are fit and well whenever we are able to get away from the hotel for a ride. In his kitchen, Simon and I chat as we look out of his windows over the bleak winter landscape and discuss the horses' menu while outside, Jeanette saddles up Abby ready for me to go out.

Just walking into the horse's stable, with the smell of straw and hay, to be greeted in anticipation by the animal, relaxes me. Rubbing Abby's soft nose and calmly chatting about my day's frustrations slowly brings me back to reality. There is nothing so good for the inside of man than the outside of a horse. Once I am up on Abby's back and in the saddle I begin to feel much better. We roll along the quiet lanes and look at the world from a different perspective. We see winter nudging its way towards an early spring. I begin to notice the delicate early primroses and snowdrops. This month the land around the Island is completely saturated with water. It has been a bad winter for the farmers but with the unnaturally mild temperatures spring is forcing itself out too early. Hedgehogs have woken up and the pretty red squirrels, native to and prolific around the Island, are darting everywhere across our path. Hold back, hold back, I want to shout. Once out in the countryside we pick up speed and have a steady canter. The air rushes over my face and my eyes begin to water as the sure-footed mare dodges the puddles along the track. My head clears and nature fills me with her tonic.

The other thing I do when the stress becomes unbearable is to stare out to sea. Since my childhood it has been a way of calming down. How lucky we are to live so close to it. Today the sea is steely grey and flat, but so often at this time of year it is violent with movement and spray. An awesome sight which certainly puts human problems in perspective. I suffer when I am away from the sea or water for long periods. When I lived in London I had to regularly return to the Island at the weekends. Now, as I get up, every day I appreciate living in a beautiful stone house, in a picture-postcard street, twenty-five yards from the sea.

As I return from the ride I think there is something very stoic in the character of people who choose to live on an island. Britain is an island, I know, but on the Isle of Wight you really know you are isolated from the mainland. Its unsophisticated charms have throughout its long history attracted all types of people from British monarchs to simple miners, literary giants to Richard Noble and his team who developed the fastest car in the world, Thrust II. It seems as if nearly everyone in southern England has visited it once on a school outing, if only to go to Alum Bay and the Needles to collect the coloured sand. Some have then returned with their children or in their twilight years to retire to its rolling hills and tiny creeks. Much of the Island's countryside is designated an Area of Outstanding Natural Beauty. Caught in a time warp, the Island has great appeal and, separated from the mainland by the waters of the Solent, seems aloof from change and all that is contemporary.

On a clear day you can almost see the face of the clock on Portsmouth town hall from Ryde esplanade. But in the midst of a force-nine gale Ryde could be hundreds of miles from the nearest land. When I was a child the tubby, round passenger ferries with their ocean-liner funnels would plough back and forth, come rain or shine. The six-mile crossing took over thirty minutes. Down below deck was a warm wooden bar dispensing everything from Scotch whisky to Scotch eggs but mostly what Dylan Thomas described as 'liquorice bog-black tea' steaming from an enormous pot. The boat had a selection of lounges down below and extraordinarily uncomfortable seats doubling as lifebuoys spread around the open upper decks. Rusty and smelly though they were, these old ferries were nonetheless sturdy, reliable and much loved. Even in the strongest storms they continued to ply their way between Portsmouth harbour and the pier head at Ryde. On one foggy winter night a ferry hit the pier, leaving a great gap which swallowed up one of the local taxis. In the height of the summer season the old paddle steamer would come out. Incredibly slow and very rusty, she flapped her way across in the warmer months. The crossing was a holiday in itself.

Then there were the old car ferries. You had to beware where you parked on a stormy day, as a saltwater car wash was common on board. The catering facilities were less hospitable than on the passenger ferries but the bar always had the odd local propping up the far end and ready to tell one and all some yarn. The car ferry took even longer, anything up to an hour from Portsmouth and as much as an hour and a half from Southampton. The run that was (and still is) the quickest and the prettiest, is between Yarmouth harbour and Lymington, a lovely journey with the north-west coast and the Needles in the distance and through the reed banks and sailing boats of the Lymington estuary.

In the sixties, along with the infamous Isle of Wight pop festival and visits from legends like the Beatles, Jimmy Hendrix and Bob Dylan, the hovercraft arrived, immortalised in a local folk song as 'the rumbling Westland SRN supersonic hovercraft'. What an invention it proved to be, and a boon to the Island. It reduced the journey time from thirty minutes to ten and whizzed along on a cushion of air between Ryde and Southsea. People still marvel that the Isle of Wight is only a simple journey of less than two hours from central London.

Now we are blessed with a choice of six different fast and frequent services with a ferry leaving on average every eight minutes from one of the four mainland ports. There is much talk of a bridge or tunnel which would be a disaster for the Island. The three different ferry operators, Wightlink, Red Funnel Ferries and Hovertravel, have crossings from as far apart as Southsea in the East to Lymington in the west, covering nearly thirty miles along the south coast of England. They disembark on the north side of the Island from Yarmouth in the west to Ryde in the east. Three different car ferry crossing routes work in conjunction with two high-speed ferries and the hovercraft. The problem is that the cost of all the crossings appear high in comparison to the cost of Channel ferry fares (highly discounted since the opening of the Channel Tunnel) and some believe if we had a tunnel or bridge it would reduce the price. Maybe – I have seen the figures and I am not convinced. The tunnel operators could hold the Island to ransom far more than the three ferry operators. Apart from anything else, the tunnel would cause long delays on both sides and actually offer fewer options than the numerous ports of departure we have at the moment. I am convinced that a great part of the attraction of the Isle of Wight is the strip of water that separates it from the mainland. We need to promote the benefits of living on such an exclusive piece of land just off the coast of England, not try to join up and become another Hayling Island whose bridge to the mainland at Portsmouth has caused terrible traffic problems and loss of all its individuality. This view is not popular with commercial operators and the business community, but I still believe very strongly that although a fixed link would not be detrimental to us and our business it would destroy the way of life I so deeply cherish.

On returning to the hotel at night to view the new restaurant in full swing, I am horrified to discover the room shrouded in blackness. Nick, perhaps under the influence of the lunchtime power-cut, has got over-excited with the new dimmer switch. The poor guests are sitting in semi-darkness and I can't imagine how they have been able to read the menus without a torch. I say nothing but disappear into the office and wait until the end of service. I have had to learn to hold my tongue. I return to the new restaurant and indicate with a black marker pen exactly how dimmed we want the lights. Teething problems!

We removed one of the two swing in/out doors between kitchen and restaurant in order to make room for a much requested *espresso* machine.

Having only one door, however, could cause problems, especially as there's a step immediately in front of it. I fall down on the first day and I expect all the service staff have as well. But it can only get better with time (I hope), and in the meantime I chase up the large black-and-yellow 'trip hazard' warning signs and pin up notices everywhere on the kitchen side to remind us to mind the step! The great advantage to the single door is that we have cut out much of the unwanted noise from the kitchen. With walls of stainless steel and over a dozen people working in a confined space under pressure, their voices can easily penetrate the hushed atmosphere of the dignified restaurant. There have been moments of acute embarrassment when a dear old lady's order has been taken against the overheard background description of a young chef's laddish exploits the night before.

Nick and I train all the staff who work at the Seaview to constantly check with the guests to ensure they have everything they need and are enjoying their stay or meal. We had noted before we changed the restaurant that several guests didn't like the corner table nearest the kitchen. They found it too noisy – a shame, since it was a great position from which to people-watch. Now with sound-proofing, fitted booth seats and a new glass partition, it has suddenly become one of our best tables. It is so satisfying when you can turn a disadvantage into an advantage.

Following my London trip to Peter Jones in the autumn, we have covered all the old dining chairs in a rich navy blue material so that even the staff think I have bought new chairs. Each table has its new thick velvet undercloth, with a white linen tablecloth on top. The curtain material, all fire-proofed and interlined, looks rich and dramatic with its navy and peacock blue swags and tails hanging against the terracotta walls. I like the effect and am delighted when guests remark on it.

I sit at the new table, quiet behind its booth in the corner, and gaze into the room. It is so small and yet has wined and dined a countless variety of people, some of them at interesting times in their lives. Charles Falconer, Tony Blair's old flatmate, came to visit us one weekend in May with his entire family. He was plain Mr Falconer then. Shortly after his stay he became Sir Charles Falconer, and now he's a Lord. We get Opposition party members as well, like Sir Norman Fowler and the Bottomleys who live in the village. We toe no party lines – a good hotelier or restaurateur cannot afford to. There have been journalists, broadcasters, writers and actors. Anna Ford, Melvyn Bragg, Roald Dahl, Simon Callow, Joanna Lumley, Sir Alec Guinness, George Melly, Thora Hird, Elaine Paige, Helena Bonham-Carter, Princesss Diana's mother Frances Shand Kydd, Lord Richard Attenborough, Jo Brand and many, many more – even Nipper, the dog from HMV. I'm embarrassed to name-drop but it's a privilege to do so since they all visit the Seaview.

We need to preserve our unique atmosphere at the Seaview while constantly trying to improve and redecorate. When we built the new Sunshine Restaurant at the back of the hotel in 1996, it transformed the place. The clean, simple lines and modern space gave us a stylish, contemporary look which evolved into the sort of restaurant you find in London or the South of France. Now we have brought the old established hotel restaurant at the front into line. I knew I needed to keep much of the old-fashioned warmth and style, and we managed to achieve that while still altering the décor and lighting. Instead of everyone wanting to eat in the Sunshine Restaurant at the back, they will all want to come to the front now. Saturday night, and the lighting is good. Hands off, Nick.

Since returning from our holiday I am looking at the possibility of setting up a web site for the hotel. Both Nick and I, though not Luddites, find running a small business in the midst of a technological revolution very hard. Nick only recently mastered the video machine! I went back to college a few years ago and am reasonably competent on the basics of the computer (I communicate with the children by daily email), but a web site costing thousands of pounds to set up and maintain does worry us. I have contacted a young man called Mark Tindall from Newmedia Internet Communications and he is coming to see me. The information he has already sent on email is confusing and I wonder if it is all necessary. We did try a computerised booking system once but, finding it less flexible for the very small operator like us, we reverted to our chart with the rooms allocated in pencil. Being able simply to rub things out and add on seems to work for us, but I will keep an open mind about Mark's web site and wait to hear what he can suggest.

We travel up to Norfolk one Sunday night in late January for our first annual meeting since we became members of the Great Inns of England. Simon Bell is the creative writer for the group's publicity. I am amused by his description of the other twelve members and I wonder how he will view the Seaview. I soon read what he has to say, after he heard the story of Nick failing to keep an appointment with a lady who wanted to discuss the plans for her forthcoming wedding at the hotel. Nick had left for a short sailing race an hour earlier and was becalmed at sea. Along with the fact that our house is a bank (once a Lloyds branch) complete with vault full of double magnums of Chateau Petrus, he wrote the following:

Islands can be strange places. Whole species get stranded on them, existing nowhere else on Earth. Nick and Nicky Hayward are living proof of this. For a start, you wonder whether Nick actually exists at all. When you ask Nicky where Nick is, the answer is invariably, 'He's becalmed,' or 'He's lashed to the tiller.' Could it be that Nicky is a tragic woman who's invented her husband? In fact, Nicky seduced Nick in The Seaview and modestly gave the credit to the breakfast in bed. It was clearly so phenomenal they bought the entire hotel and have now won enough awards to earn a slipped disc. They live in a bank, its vaults full of Château Petrus, and play host to admirals and stokers. It could be said the Haywards carry on an Island tradition – wrecking – except that The Seaview is a place you'd want to be wrecked in, as it were. Whether it's the local seafood in one of their excellent restaurants, a spot of five-star seduction, or simply peering out to sea looking for Nick, The Seaview has the charm, beauty, style, cosiness and sheer curiosity to satisfy all legal tastes.

It's a rather different approach but we think it's great fun. We are reassured when we meet up with the other members of the Great Inns – not only do all of them have similar operations to ourselves but they share our sense of humour, along with many of our business beliefs. One of the hotels is the Rising Sun at Lynmouth in Devon where Hugo and Pam Jeune not only know what it is like to work in a sixteen-bedroomed inn next to the sea but also keep horses for relaxation. Then we meet Sir Thomas and Lady Ingilby, owners of the Boar's Head at Ripley in North Yorkshire, and discover we have mutual friends from the old days when we lived in London. We have a fruitful and constructive meeting before heading back to the Island.

A phone call one afternoon from Jeremy Howell, the local BBC South reporter. The Isle of Wight Council has a shortfall in their health budget. One of the Island's many social problems is that with over 27 per cent of the population retired and on a limited income, health resources are easily drained and it now seems that the politicians' latest solution is to tax tourists. Jeremy wants to know my reaction. Outraged, is the answer. I cannot believe that an island which relies so heavily on tourism is proposing to tax people just for the benefit of stepping on to our shores. I splutter down the phone at Jeremy and he asks to come over and film an interview. That night I appear on the local news, indignantly suggesting that this tax is sending out totally the wrong signal. A few locals come in and congratulate me on my performance, but I am rather embarrassed as the camera lighting seems to have gone wrong and I look as pink as Miss Piggy and about as outraged. Maybe my temper needs a dimmer.

In spite of the terrible weather and sodden ground we have the first of the meetings to organise the Isle of Wight Grand National. Nick is chairing the committee this year and all the meetings take place on a Monday night in our house. Up until the mid 1920s there was a race course in a field at Ashey. It was particularly popular during the late nineteenth century when Queen Victoria would arrive at Ashey station in her private train, which was then backed on to the course for her to use as a private box. Towards the end of its life the course developed an infamous reputation and was described as the most corrupt race course in the country. The story goes that when the jockeys

disappeared behind a small copse the horses sometimes changed position – and colour too. The
grandstand at Ashey was burnt down in the
twenties under suspicious circumstances (an early
false insurance claim, perhaps).

Seven years ago a small group put forward a
proposal for holding a one-day meeting on the old
ground. With our natural love of horses and riding
we were asked to help and to sponsor the event.
Over the years it has grown and now many local
businesses club together and with a team of
enthusiastic volunteers turn a brown muddy field
into a race course for the day. That requires quite a
bit of organisation, hence the numerous meetings.
It has been suggested that Meridian Television's
Great Day Out programme might feature the event.
I call them up and yes, they like the idea and pencil
in the date – a Sunday just before Easter. The committee, meanwhile, needs to give them more
details. There is plenty more planning to go into the
day. Who will run the car park? Will the IOW Pony
Club ladies still do all the food ? With the ground so
waterlogged is there any chance of it drying out in
time ?

A week after the opening of the new front
restaurant the door falls off its hinges. It chooses to
do so when the restaurant is full. The entire hotel is
full but had anyone been upstairs they might have
heard a small clunk. The noise and brilliant neon
light of the kitchen soon invades the dining room's
atmosphere. We are in the middle of the second of
our wine tastings. Fifty guests are sampling their

way through the delicious wines brought down from London by Nick Strachan of Mentzendorff, the tasting to be followed by our carefully selected menu and accompanying wines. My sense of humour quickly fades like a shallow wine with a short finish. David tries to go out into the restaurant but cannot move the door either way. Luckily, having swung off its hinge, the door blocks shut, keeping out the kitchen light and noise, but making it impossible to serve the food. We have to take each plate out by the office and walk down the corridor, entering the restaurant through the customers' entrance. It works. And, as with so many of our dramas, hardly anyone notices and fortune chooses to smile on us again.

The next day at breakfast we jokingly explain to the guests that Barry the carpenter, currently on his knees trying to rehang the door, has been specially laid on by the hotel as their early-morning entertainment. No one minds People usually don't if you explain to them rather than hide misfortune. Barry discovers that one of the screws holding the door hinge snapped. Another one, larger and stronger this time, is driven home and all is back to normal. The door will have to cope with a lot of swinging when the restaurant is full so we decide to add an extra reinforcement just in case.

Despite the door incident the wine tasting is a huge success. We have bought wines from Mentzendorff since we first bought the Seaview, initially because they are the agents for Bollinger champagne. When I was at Corney & Barrow,

Keith Stevens the chairman, a delightful, lugubrious old boy, was trained by Madame Bollinger. I was taught at an early age that it was one of the few non-vintage champagnes that would mature with a delightful nutty flavour. Now Nick Strachan, who knows Seaview well as his wife's family live in the village, shows a selection of Mentzendorff wines with our special menu.

1999 WINTER WINE TASTING

Friday 29th January 1999

Nick Strachan from Mentzendorff
presenting a selection of wines
followed by dinner

Smoked Haddock & Scrambled Egg on Toasted Muffin

Pouilly-Fuissé, Joseph Drouhin 1996

Calves' Liver with Bacon & Sage mash &
Deep-fried Sage & Red Onions

Château Moulin de Duhart, Pauillac 1995

Pancakes with Orange & Grand Marnier

Fresh Coffee with Island cream & mints

Fonseca Bin 27

Total price £27.50
per person including VAT @ 17.5%
including the tasting, dinner & all dinner wines

The menu proves to be a difficult one to produce on the night. Cooking over fifty portions of calves' liver to order for a function is not an experience which either Charlie or I will repeat. Single orders at a time would have been fine but calves' liver is not good when mass-produced. Cooking for large parties and functions like our regular tasting dinners is so different from preparing normal restaurant food. When an old restaurateur friend of ours had his society wedding dinner at Terence Conran's restaurant, Quaglino's in St James's, expectations were high. Unfortunately, this smart restaurant, one that can easily produce hundreds of different meals over a period of several hours, found it very hard to produce the same meal for everyone at the same time. To do this is a completely different operation from routine restaurant cooking and really needs a different kitchen. Much of the food has to be prepared beforehand so that when the time comes for twenty or forty or a hundred first courses to be taken out all in one go, with just a few finishing touches, all the plates are ready within seconds of each other. It requires expert planning and timing, lots of staff and most important, plenty of space. In our tiny engine room, with a limited number of chefs, we have to be very careful about every function menu. This time the results are delicious but far too hard and stressful for Charlie and the kitchen staff. We would have been better having a meat that didn't need to be individually flash-fried to order at the last minute. Next time we will do rack of lamb with a fresh herb crust.

A few days later we face another interesting evening. Somehow, Nick has overbooked the restaurants, a very uncommon thing for him to do. In London hotels, overbooking is common because of 'no shows' – people who book accommodation or restaurant tables and then simply don't show up. When Nick was at the Royal Garden, they had to 'book out' (send to another hotel) a whole coachload. We never overbook at the Seaview – it is too stressful. On any given day you can be reasonably sure that someone will drop out, but when you overbook, you gamble on that definitely happening. Nick and I are not gamblers.

Now Nick has accepted a local dinner function for fifty-odd in the Sunshine Restaurant, plus a private party for nearly twenty. Where are we going to put them all? On the ceiling? It's too cold for dining al fresco. To add to our problems, the hotel bedrooms are unusually busy and all the guests want to eat in the dining room. After some quick thinking, we turn the front bar into a private dining room for the party of twenty, setting up one large square table, coated in linen, silver and glass, in the middle of the room with five settings down each side. With the lights dimmed down and the table covered in candles and surrounded by the fascinating old naval pictures, the room looks great. Then we just have to sort out the residents – they can all eat in the new front restaurant (preferably with a working door). I will then stand at the front door, quietly directing each guest to their slot, appease any regulars who feel excluded from the front bar, and coax them down to the pub at the back. Will it be OK? We worry. We plan. We'll see. We set up the rooms and try to ensure that every party will have more than they expect. We have written to each of the incoming guests explaining that the hotel has two private parties on, but that they can eat either in the new front restaurant or in the bar around the fire with the locals. We hope we have done enough to give them comfort. On the night, everyone seems happy. All goes surprisingly well, though I feel as if I am directing traffic in Piccadilly Circus. We do over a hundred and six covers on a wet January night, and no complaints.

The next day I am on the horse again to soothe away some of the tension. Then it's back to prepare our speech for the hotel conference down in Falmouth tomorrow. I need to relax as a very busy January comes to a close.

CHAPTER 5

February
Conferences and Parties

A visit to old friends. We stop off on our way to the hotel conference in Cornwall to stay with Robin and Louella Hanbury-Tenison, who have recently branched out into the bed-and-breakfast business of a high-class kind. Robin is an author, explorer, TV celebrity and past leader of the Countryside Alliance. Now he is also helping Louella host their Cornish B&B operation in the unique farmhouse they have painstakingly restored.

I first met Louella in London in the early seventies and, through both our marriages and first children, we kept in regular contact until Nick and I moved to the Island. We then lost touch except for the odd Christmas card. Two years ago Louella and Robin came to the Island when he was the main speaker at a special dinner held in Yarmouth for the Countryside Alliance. It was such a pleasure to see her again and to catch up on one another's news. We vowed not to lose touch again. Since then, we have met skiing, and last summer I went down to Cornwall with Pip and Jules for a couple of blissfully quiet days during the busy summer season.

Now Nick, too, is visiting their farm, tucked picturesquely into Bodmin Moor. He adores their house. I knew he would. He was brought up on a farm in Devon and the West Country feels like home to him. The peace and solitude of the break and our time with Robin and Louella makes for a rare respite.

In the sixties Robin took part in an unusual and difficult expedition to South America, travelling in a hovercraft (manufactured on the Isle of Wight) up uncharted waters of the Amazon River. The journey was captured on a documentary film and Robin wrote a book about his adventures. I remember the excitement on the Island about the potential of hovercraft to master any terrain or waterway, exemplified on this bracing journey. During our stay in Cornwall Robin produces his book documenting the adventure and recalls the dangers and excitements of his travels. We also watch a preview of Robin's latest Channel 4 documentary, a poignant programme about his returning, after nearly twenty years, to a remote tribe in Borneo.

Then it's up to our magnificent bedroom complete with a copy of *Hello!* magazine, featuring the Hanbury-Tenisons at home. Louella, always sensitive to detail and taking good care of guests, runs a smart operation and I am sure all her visitors feel special. We certainly did.

Next day we move on to the hotel conference in Falmouth. Nick and I have been asked to give another presentation – 'Profiting from Awards'. Jeremy Willcock is the owner of the George Hotel at the other end of the Island, in Yarmouth. We were delighted when the Willcocks, a highly professional and charming couple moved to the Island in 1994, if somewhat envious as the George was the one hotel we had always wanted to own. Knowing it needed major capital investment, we never had enough money and were too scared to take on a large bank loan. Jeremy was able to plough in a huge investment and bring the elegant old hotel, steeped in history, up to a very high standard.

Jeremy is also the chairman of the Consort Hotel Group, a marketing and purchasing consortium consisting of a group of small hotels. Consort was about to merge with Best Western Hotels, to make the largest group of independent hotels in the UK. Over the years, we have worked with the George on a number of promotions and it seemed, on the face of it, sensible to join the scheme as well. But large groups and company branding is not for us, we feel. Our main fear is that we might lose our identity and, with it, our fierce independence. Nick had worked for a large group before and knows the perils. I am very much the small independent hotelier and would not dream of having it any other way. Neither of us wants or likes someone telling us what to do in our own hotel.

The conference proves different from anything we have experienced before. Many of the members are former Trust House Forte managers and all seem content to be in large groups. With plenty of jargon flying around, they speak the same management language. I learn new things, particularly from the restaurant section of the Automobile Association who give a talk on what inspectors look

public know and understand about the hotel industry. People neither comprehend nor care about grading schemes like stars, let alone crowns, percentages, commendations, ribbons or rosettes. People have fixed ideas about big chains, especially Trust House Forte, and understand even less about consortiums of hotels like Consort or Best Western. I know the marketing people say branding is all-important, but part of me thinks people just want best care. You can have as many gongs as you like but if you don't give constant high standards and a friendly, personal service they won't keep coming back.

Nick and I have one or two very close friends in the hotel industry, but we are not very sociable and definitely not natural 'networkers' at trade functions and conference gatherings. We both hate the word 'networking'. We believe that people want a unique experience when they come to small individual hotels like the Seaview. Having recently attended the hoteliers' dinner in Evesham with Hilary Rubinstein, and the meeting of members of the Great Inns of England, we find ourselves mixing with other members of the industry far more than we have ever done before. We are not sure this is good for us. We try to keep an open mind, especially as it is becoming increasingly hard for the small independent operator to survive in this industry. But we are determined that the Seaview will not lose its hard-won identity.

Now we are to stand up in front of a few of our corporate peers and spout forth on the benefits of

taking part in awards. It's scary, although we have
prepared well and keep reading our speech aloud
beforehand, for practice. Our main fear is that no
one will turn up. Unfortunately, we're on parade
first thing in the morning, following a grand gala
dinner the night before. We left the revels reasonably early, but gather it then went on all night. We
prepare the small conference room for our talk and
wait, in pathetic isolation. Then a few people show
up, including Jeremy's wife Amy, and by the time
we're ready to begin a small group has assembled.

I think it goes well. One man asks me afterwards
where I get my energy. I never think we do all that
much but they all seem amazed at what we pack
into our day and ask lots of questions. We have
been approached to speak at a number of larger
events over the next few weeks and months, so we
are delighted that this went well and feel more
confident about presentations in public.

As we drive home we're both fired with new ideas
for the hotel, especially what we need to do in the
restaurant. We don't have a boardroom at the
Seaview and much of our future planning takes
place, like now, on long car journeys. We decide to
look for a property near the Seaview that could
alleviate the problem of our limited hotel space and
accommodation. Especially after hearing about the
successful annexe both at the Hoste Arms in
Burnham Market and the Wykeham Arms in
Winchester. When we get home, we discover, to
our complete surprise, that Myrtle Cottage, a tiny
two-hundred-year-old fisherman's cottage built on

the side of the hotel, is on the market for £60,000. We put in an offer and it's accepted. Well, well. We'll see what happens.

Pip's eighteenth birthday is this month. Trying to give her the party she wants and we can afford is not easy. We left London partly to give our children a better quality of life, but running your own small business is very demanding and frequently the children are deprived of time and attention. There is sometimes a tendency by successful working parents to try to overcompensate with material things. So Nick and I try hard to maintain a reasonable balance. Pip decides she would like a small dinner in London on the weekend of her birthday and insists that her father has to be there, even if it does mean missing a busy Saturday night at the hotel. As the following day is St Valentine's, we know we will have to get back to the business quickly to welcome all the dining lovers. Pip's 'Tiara & DJ dinner party' is held at Launceston Place Restaurant in Kensington. Young girls in glamorous gowns and glitzy headpieces, accompanied by crisp young men in black and white, arrive for the champagne reception which our friend Simon Slater has organised, followed by a delicious dinner. Then all the young disappear to party away the night at Richard Branson's Kensington Roof Garden, complete with pink flamingos. For Nick and I to be away from the hotel on a Saturday night requires considerable organisation, making sure we have sufficient cover both day and night. We are not off duty though. While in London we have to buy new letterboxes for three rooms outside the hotel (so we can deliver daily newspapers without disturbing the guests), new bedspreads and a heavy outside door stop. All this along with girls' hairdos and daddy taking his grown-up daughter off to buy a new dress. That night after the dinner, Nick and I retire reasonably early in the London flat. Only to be woken at regular intervals as merry offspring return or, in Ben's case, turn up at 3am and leave again at 6am to catch the Eurostar back to university in Bordeaux. In the morning we leave London as bleary-eyed as our children, but with no time to catch up on our sleep as the next excitement is the hotel's special Valentine's night dinner.

Normally the hotel restaurants are closed on a Sunday night but this year St Valentine's falls on a Sunday. We remain open for a special dinner and package break that includes a romantic overnight stay. The hotel is full of romantics both young and old and, having missed Saturday night, we need to return to welcome the lovers. Fifty in the restaurant plus thirty-two staying on in the sixteen rooms.

All the beds are made up as doubles, some with the new bedspreads from London. We recently replaced many of the beds with special zip-and-link beds which can either be made up into two separate twin beds or put together to make one very large double. Charlie has created a special menu and we have specifically kept the price low. We adopt a similar policy on a number of evenings in the winter to encourage those who might not normally use the hotel to take advantage of the special price. One couple, who don't know that the hotel restaurant is normally shut on a Sunday, write later to say they were disappointed with the limited special menu and wanted to dine à la carte with more choice. Nick explains the special circumstances and invites them back at the hotel's expense on a normal evening. They are delighted.

VALENTINE'S SPECIAL DINNER
Sunday 14th February 1999

Hot Goats' Cheese & Spinach Mousse

Pan-fried breast of Chicken, with cream,
wild & field mushrooms
Selection of fresh vegetables

Floating Islands with praline & crème anglaise

Fresh Filter Coffee with Island cream & mints

Total cost of Special Valentine's Dinner £16.50
per person including VAT @ 17.5%

Over the years, we have watched a number of romances blossom at the hotel, some culminating in marriage, some amongst our own staff. Charlie married Helen after she came to work as a chef and Steve, a young manager, married Valerie from the reception. Angela is currently being courted by Russell, an excellent electrician from Berry

Electrics – this no doubt began after he rewired her computer. We also have older regular couples who have used the hotel to celebrate silver or ruby anniversaries. It is a privilege and tremendous pleasure in this trade to watch and help others happily commemorate their special day. We try to ensure we give a particularly personalised service, printing out special menus with their names and providing a card from Nick and me and a special cake, in fact almost everything – including acting as unofficial photographers. So Valentine's evening is a joy to watch.

It's hard for clandestine lovers in these modern times. Hotel and restaurant staff have to be very discreet. Computerised booking systems that use credit and swipe cards, not to mention the perils of being put on mailing lists, means that illicit liaisons in small country hotels or pubs are hard to keep secret now. Mr & Mrs Smith, checking in off the street and paying in advance with cash are a thing of the past, and nowadays would even arouse great suspicion. Lovers have to meet in motorway Travel Inns and Lodges – functional but hardly romantic. This is a very sensitive area of our business. Nick remembers in London how managers had to be very prudent, never confusing wives with mistresses. One gentleman insisted on having both his wife and mistress staying in the hotel at the same time. Each was oblivious to the other. Thrilled by the excitement of his deception remaining undiscovered (thanks very much to the tact of the entire hotel staff), he then arrived with a third woman!

That was a bit much. The entire affair ended in catastrophe when an irate husband turned up and the whole charade was rumbled.

We had an embarrassing incident at the Seaview once when Nick gave a cheery welcome back to a man who had stayed with us a few days earlier. He glared at Nick and assured him that he had never set foot in the hotel before. Thinking fast, Nick realised the man was with a different woman. You need a good memory in this game.

Ploughing up and down the lanes of the swimming pool in Ryde early one February morning I think about the visit of Allan Willett, the newly appointed boss of the SEEDA, the South East England Development Agency, our region's section of the government's Regional Development Agency. Allan is no stranger to the hotel, having wined and dined here with friends in the past. The Island is like many other impoverished regions bidding for special aid at both the UK and European level. In his new capacity, he is now seen by many local agencies as an important and influential figure for the future of the Island. Our local council, in partnership with the private sector, wants to ensure that he fully understands the Isle of Wight's needs and aspirations and grasps the complexity of the problems and difficulties facing our community.

Everyone is very excited and we've had numerous telephone calls, faxes and letters regarding the requirements for his visit, some from the SEEDA offices in Guildford, some from our local authority, some from the local Island Regeneration Partnership, and other instructions from board members in the private sector. Unfortunately the two Island representatives who made the original booking for Allan and his entourage are away on holiday. It is very confusing for the hotel reception: as one mainland agency adds another room, so someone else cancels. We know they choose the hotel because of our reputation for efficient professionalism, but with all the changes we feel under real pressure and all the staff are nervous.

The guest of honour and numerous supporting bodies arrive at the Seaview promptly at 5.45. Nick and I are at the door waiting to greet the Willett entourage, escorting them to their rooms and organising refreshments. They quickly settle in before rushing off to an official dinner at the Royal Yacht Squadron in Cowes. I have also been invited.

The Royal Yacht Squadron is an extraordinary institution, with an exclusively male membership, and steeped in history, etiquette and strict rules. As an Islander and non-member, it is a great honour to be swanning in through the front gates. I am slightly nervous as I'm alone and can't quite remember the details but know the ladies' entrance is at the side. Usually only members with male guests use the main door. Women use the side entrance to the club and there is a separate ladies' staircase to the bedrooms upstairs. I am told this rule was originally made in order to ensure that members' partners, whether wives or mistresses, could enter discreetly. Along with most Islanders and the hoi polloi, I usually viewed the club only from the outside looking in. I first entered 'The Castle', as it is known to the members, when I was working for Corney & Barrow, who supplied wine not only in London but also to a few discerning provincial clubs. The Royal London Yacht Club bought their house wine from Corney & Barrow for years and so, through Mike Gardener, its chief steward, I was invited into the Squadron. The secretary, Robin Rising, showed me round and I particularly remember their very impressive cellars.

Since then Nick and I have been invited in for several events including the Squadron Ball in 1997. It was the Royal Yacht *Britannia*'s last year in Cowes and the ball took place on a hot August evening. Christopher Bland, an old family friend, had just become Lord Lieutenant of the Isle of Wight and invited us to join his party. As we looked out over a calm sea, the floodlit lines of the *Britannia* dominated the harbour. Among the many distinguished guests on the dance floor were the Princess Royal, the Duke of Edinburgh, Prince Edward, the Kents and various other royals. I wondered what they thought about *Britannia* being decommissioned and destined to end its life as a floating function room in Scotland. What a comedown for the majestic old ship. As somebody from the Island where she had so many links, I was deeply saddened by her fate, but on that particular night I felt honoured to watch her last bedecked and bejewelled appearance in Cowes in such privileged circumstances.

Now here I am, back at the exclusive club, chatting before dinner. We go into the private members' dining room and I wonder about all the events and discussions that have taken place here. The dark panelled walls are covered with maritime paintings and gleaming yachting trophies. In the middle a huge U-shaped table is perfectly laid for a formal dinner. I sit at the far end of one of the large wing tables and watch the staff serving the meal impeccably; just out of sight I can hear them chatting quietly about tonight's company. Having served on monarchs with dignity, they are clearly not impressed by this gathering. I turn my attention to the speeches and wonder what this latest action will do for the future of the Island.

Next day the meetings continue with a special Tourism breakfast group at the Seaview. Not quite the Squadron but we put on a good show. The front bar is laid out like a boardroom with a large table in the middle for the meeting. Nick is in charge of the hotel side while I join the breakfast group. I try hard to listen and concentrate instead of focusing on two croissants with burnt black corners that I can see clearly in front of me. I do my bit and say my tuppenceworth, stressing the importance the government now places on hospitality as a fast-growing industry. Having been a member of the main government tourism forum since its formation in 1996 (after the Seaview came top of the benchmarking on small hotels), and having worked closely with the Department of Culture, Media and Sport under Chris Smith, I have personally been involved in the creation of an official document called *Tomorrow's Tourism*. At the same time, I try to catch Nick's eye, to get him to remove the offending pastries.

Allan Willett suggests after breakfast that I might take a role in the new tourism sector group to be formed by the Regional Development Agency. I feel flattered, but also worried about exactly what I'm being asked to do and how much time it will involve. It has been interesting for the Seaview to be highlighted as an example of best practice both as employer and as a small, privately run business. But freely devoting days to travel to London or Guildford to attend meetings, at our expense, to provide an example of small business, benefits . . . I'm not sure who. It can be exhausting and can detract from my input to the running of the Seaview.

Everyone whizzes off for their helicopter tour of the Island as Nick and I breathe a sigh of relief, get out of our formal clothes and head off to ride our horses over the downs. It is, after all, meant to be our day off.

Winter is almost over. I can't believe where the time has gone. When we first bought the hotel winters stretched on for ever. Bars and beaches were deserted and any sign of snow and freezing conditions spelled disaster since it meant cancelled bookings. This year has been wet, with virtually no snow. There has been the odd quiet period in the hotel but never for long, and Nick and I are finding it hard to take off even one day a week. We have lost our high and low periods and there is little time to rest and recuperate.

Fay, in housekeeping, cannot even find time to shut off rooms for spring-cleaning or decorating. Each year every room is closed for several days. Two or three are completely gutted and refurbished every three to four years, but all the others are stripped and cleaned. All the curtains and bed-spreads, blankets and cushions are sent off to the cleaners. The furniture is piled in the middle of the room and the paint and woodwork is washed and polished from floor to ceiling. Sometimes there are small details to attend to or some decorating touching-up to do. Around the bath in Room 17 we have had constant problems with a patch of black mould, so we strip off and replace all the tiles. We discover the wood behind the bath is rotten so there is more to be done than we anticipated. We cut out all the rot and damp and replace with new wood before adding sparkling new tiles around the bath.

Recent research by the Confederation of British Industry discovered that what consumers most want to find in hotels is not twenty-four-hour coffee shops, swimming pools, saunas, or hundreds of fancy gadgets in the rooms, but simply a warm friendly welcome and, top priority, clean bath-rooms. We try hard to provide both at the Seaview.

Accepting dogs at the hotel can put an added responsibility on the housekeeping. I have to admit that Nick and I are very dog-friendly people. (We have two of our own.) We welcome all dogs, though, Millie sometimes gets very territorial and can take a violent dislike to some visiting canines, or sometimes even arriving guests. I once found her protesting vociferously, at the top of her bark, at an eminent high court judge who was forced to fend her off with his newspaper. Now we avoid Millie as part of the welcome at the Seaview.

We ask dog owners to bring their pet's bedding and not to allow them on our soft furnishings. We have our regulars like Oscar, a small pug, who visited every summer and had Charlie prepare his favourite dish, a little lightly poached chicken breast. Oscar was not a fit dog. He rarely walked more than a few paces and preferred to be carried around by his owner in a shopping basket on wheels. When the dogs check out we have to ensure that the rooms are meticulously cleaned before showing in the next guest, who may not appreciate following a canine occupant.

It is, however, often easier to clean a room after a visit from an animal than a heavy smoker. There is just no way of getting rid of the smell of smoke, though we invest heavily in all the advertised products. This year we are introducing two non-smoking rooms especially for guests who really cannot bear the smell of stale fumes.

The other horror for housekeeping staff is artistically inspired children with felt-tip pens. Parents who would never allow their offspring to mark bedspreads or walls at home surprisingly fail to be as conscientious when their children decide to be creative in a hotel. No amount of dry-cleaning can remove the mark of a permanent felt-tip and we are forced to leave the stain until we can replace the material. Housekeeping also has to deal with many accidents – in the beds, on carpets, almost any-where in the room. We have even had the odd unpleasant shock in the wastepaper bins, which I won't go into. Fay and her housekeeping team are amazing and always sort out things so that the room is fresh and clean for the incoming guest.

It is hard to know what each bedroom is like from the guests' point of view. Over the years members of my family, the manager and heads of department have stayed in different rooms and given us their opinion. We want continuously to improve, so we are always trying to add thoughtful touches, which, we hope, give added value. We put in many extras during the early development of the hotel – individual hand-made pincushions, for example, in every bedroom. Originally we were unable to afford the usual hotel 'give-aways', as they were expensive and we were desperately short of cash, so cut up the ancient velvet curtains in the old dining room, stuffed them with torn strips of the old lining, and added buttons, needles and pins to make hotel sewing kits at hardly any cost. Interestingly, no one has ever taken one away. More recently, we hung individual lavender bags in every wardrobe to give that lovely old-fashioned smell. When we first bought the hotel my naughty sister Annie came to stay and added a condom to every Welcome pack. We did not discover her practical joke until a couple of days later when an elderly spinster questioned Nick on the exact purpose of the small sealed packet.

Nowadays every hotel, large or small, seems to have many personal give-aways in the bedrooms. I went in to the opening of a huge new development which had previously been an old-fashioned holiday camp, and they now had executive suites with decanters of sherry and glasses on silver trays. Sometimes the competition to have extras goes too far. I think ironing boards in every room is excessive, myself. We do try to have thoughtful touches (excluding my sister's additions), but as fast as we come up with new ideas we discover hundreds of hotel bedrooms around the country are doing the same thing. But most of all we try to ensure that the rooms are spotlessly clean and that we and all the staff at the Seaview are sensitive to what any individual guest may need to make his or her stay more comfortable.

We also spring-clean all the hotel stores during the winter. Because we've been so busy, Lee, the head barman, and Charlie in the kitchen have had to sort out quiet afternoons after normal duties to have a clear-out before the summer season. All these annual jobs are so important and we have somehow to make time to do them.

Though most people think spring doesn't really start until March, it's February for us. The ground is still very wet but the Island is coming alive, ready to offer its magic to its visitors. I notice on my rides that all the bridle paths, footpaths and gates are being repaired and walks and tracks are looking very smart. The Island is holding a walking festival in May, part of the local endeavours to promote new environmentally friendly and sustainable attractions for short breaks, away from the traditional bucket-and-spade summer season. Clouds of brilliant yellow mimosa have been out for weeks and the geraniums in our garden have survived another winter. But the drier weather, although welcome, means that the council has rushed out to dig up every road on the Island to 'carry out essential works'. As we sit in the resulting traffic jams, we hope they will finish before the holiday season begins in earnest.

The Isle of Wight Grand National committee continues to meet in our house. Everyone is apprehensive about the ground, but Harold George, a local dairy farmer who is also an experienced horseman and jockey, and who is building the course, seems relaxed in spite of all the rain. I type up the entry programmes and schedules, while Nick drums up mainland competitors. With Meridian Television due to film the event, local businesses are very supportive, despite the waterlogged course. The important thing now is to get the entries – without the riders and horses, there won't be an event. Nick is to ride Abby this year, as we take it in turns to ride. I don't know why I enter, because I'm always petrified as I race round. My stomach and nerves seem to leap over the jumps before the rest of me, and I am always relieved when it's over and everyone home safely.

At the end of February Nick and I have been invited by a local friend, Anthony Goddard, to join his skiing party. We never normally have a second winter holiday, but as we are finding it increasingly difficult to discipline ourselves to take days off, we feel this break is justified. The party comprises Howard and Alison Johnson, local farmers, Brian and Kay Marriott, the partners in Marriott Design, a company we use for our brochures and artwork, the Goddards, our brewers, and ourselves. The eight Islanders set off to Val d'Isère, our second time in two months, and this time I'm not on the laptop as we drive up the mountain in a thick snowstorm. Through the blizzard we wonder what the conditions will be like for skiing. We arrive in a resort made unrecognisable by huge snowdrifts. As we collect our skis and boots, we are warned of more serious storms approaching and the risk of avalanches. The forecast is terrible and it's unlikely that we will be able to ski tomorrow. We snuggle up in our cosy chalet and listen to the wail outside.

We wake up on our first morning to discover the resort is completely cut off. The risk of a severe avalanche has increased, and everyone is warned to close windows and shutters and remain indoors – we stay glued to the radio. The next announcement tells us that the area around our chalet is in extreme danger as we are directly in the path of the last fatal avalanche, which took place here in the 1960s. Our tour company, called YSE, has moved the guests out of the neighbouring self-catering chalets. I go downstairs and find the elderly French couple who own the property in a dreadful state of panic. She begs me not to leave the chalet and explains that

7 a.m. Bringing out the front terrace furniture.

Servicing the bedrooms.

Sorting the morning newspapers.

Preparing the freshly-squeezed juice for breakfast.

Leon stocking the wine cellar.

Charlie giving orders.

Cowes yachtsmen taking early breakfast.

Paul Methuen in residence.

Olivia – one of our younger regulars.

Celebration plate to commemorate 20 years at the Seaview.

The front terrace.

Pip working in the bar.

Nicky and Charlie discussing orders.

In the heat of the kitchen.

Nick with Ben, off to teach at the Yacht Club.

Nick, Nicky, Pip and Jules.

CHAPTER 6

March
Racing and Royalty

I read through the reservations list with some alarm. March looks hectic. Every year there is a natural build-up to Easter, which this year falls in April, but the diary is already full. David Wickers, a *Sunday Times* travel journalist, arrives for the weekend with his wife and their three children. David has been good to the hotel, writing glowing articles about us, and we have used his quotes to promote the business. He once favourably called us 'the star of the British seaside'. Now a *Sunday Times* reader has nominated us for their Golden Pillow Award, so he has been sent down to confirm the recommendation. Everyone is on alert.

On the whole, travel journalists have been kind to the Seaview. It is very difficult to promote a small hotel like ours. We never advertise. The large hotel groups and chains have huge budgets and special advertising and marketing departments to promote their product. Nick and I initially had no idea how to compete, particularly since so much of our business is generated by word of mouth and returning custom. But as our reputation grew, we attracted a range of travel writers from the *Tatler* to the *Real Ale Guide*. Even Jonathan Meades, in an amusing but rude article in the *Times*, suggested that we were the best of a bad bunch on the Island, though he described our restaurant lampshades as resembling props from a clapped-out production of *Irma la Douce*. In defiance, I kept the shades for over ten years in case he came back. He never did. They were replaced this winter, though, when we redecorated the restaurant in January.

It must be hard for travel journalists constantly to review the domestic tourism market. You begin to see it like a rota system. We can usually spot hotel inspectors but journalists come in all shapes and sizes: some are voluble, some very discreet. The positive reports they have given us in national newspapers and magazines over the years have played a significant part in our success. And with the development of numerous travel programmes and consumer watchdog reports there is a different accent on publicity. Nearly every programme features both an exotic foreign destination and a domestic one. Hassles at airports and the problems of long-distance travel have made local holidays and specialised short breaks more appealing. England is suddenly in again. Places like Cornwall and the Isle of Wight are thriving in the summer. Last year Harry Enfield's father, Edward, came with his bicycle and the BBC *Holiday* programme crew to film our gourmet cycling break. We also had good coverage of our painting breaks, short off-season holidays that include specialist art classes. Breaks of an unusual kind are what people want.

Journalists, however, most often want to visit

during Cowes Week at the beginning of August and it is hard to convince them of the varied charms of the Island outside the main sailing season. A few, like David Wickers, and Susan Marling from *Good Housekeeping*, come in the spring or autumn. Both these professional travel writers dig deep, discovering the varied and interesting selection of activities that take place over any given twelve-month period. As we say goodbye to David and his family we try to be detached and objective about any criticism we may receive in his review. Secretly hoping for a good write-up, we prepare ourselves for the slings and arrows.

The Island is buzzing with the media. I find myself in the public bar chatting to a quiet man in a duffel coat accompanied by a scruffy dog, only to discover he is staying with us while searching out locations for London Weekend Television's new drama series, *Reach for the Moon*. The locals are hoping it will do for the Isle of Wight what *Bergerac* did for Jersey. At the same time a feature film is shooting in Yarmouth, and comic actor and writer Rick Mayall is also due to film on the Island. Suddenly we are photogenic.

There is a further wine tasting this month. Dennis Geal from Louis Latour was booked to come down and lecture on classic Burgundies but is taken ill. Alexander Nall stands in at the last minute as his replacement. Alexander has never met us or been to Seaview before. We are naturally all apprehensive and hoping the evening will not be a flop. Quite the contrary – Alexander is a huge success and afterwards he and Nick stay up celebrating with more tasting. As the hotel is full, Alexander is staying in our house, which sometimes houses over-flow guests who are also friends. Alexander, for-getting where he is and that he is alone, is woken during the night by what he thinks is his wife's breathing, until he realises where he is and dis-covers our dog Millie has quietly snuggled down on the pillow next to him.

We are having a new window fitted in the kitchen roof. It is necessary to alleviate some of the heat generated around the range, especially in the hot summer months. There is a good extraction system but it's very noisy and the light and fresh air from the window will improve the circulation in the kitchen during service. The problem is how to remove the stainless-steel cladding on the inside of the kitchen ceiling, remove the roof tiles and make a large hole for the new window without closing down the food service. We can't shut such an active kitchen while the window is being installed as we would then have to close the hotel.

The builders complete the work on the outside roof days before the window is installed, keeping disruption to a minimum. As usual, they perform another feat of 'gourmet' building. We temporarily rearrange the equipment and close for lunch. All goes according to plan and the new window is installed in half a day.

1998 SPRING WINE TASTING
Thursday 11th November 1999

Alexander Nall from Louis Latour
presenting a selection of White Burgundy wines
followed by dinner

Smoked Trout Terrine, white wine &
dill cream sauce with Melba Toast

Montagny 1er Cru, La Grande Roche, 1996

Venison Casserole with celeriac mash

Pinot Noir, Domaine de Valmoissine 1996

Brandy Snap Basket with red berry sorbet

Fonseca Bin 27 Port

Fresh-ground Coffee with Island cream & mints

Total price £27.50
per person including VAT @ 17.5%
including the tasting, dinner & all dinner wines

While the builders are working in the kitchen, Charlie is off for a few days with his family, while Leon the manager and Bob from the kitchen go to London to attend the annual chefs' conference. We find it is a great learning experience for members of the team to attend mainland conferences or courses and then report back to the Friday meeting at the end of the week. Both Bob and Leon return enthused by their day in London but concerned

about the future, with more food legislation loom-
ing. Genetically modified food is the latest fear but
E.coli and salmonella have also left scars among
food operators. The public is increasingly alarmed
by these scares, which does not help a flourishing
restaurant. It's so easy to have a reputation soured.
We decide to contact our suppliers and try to find
out exactly what is happening, while adding our
policy of avoiding use of all GM products to the
bottom of our menu. With details about GM, nut
allergies, smoking, mobile phones and special
dietary requirements, the menu is rather full of
warnings, health risks and nagging. Nick worries
that if the government wants us to add anything else
the warnings on the menu will take up more space
than the food.

The next event in March is Mothering Sunday
lunch. As all my children are away, I work in the
hotel as a childless mother. It's a busy day and both
the restaurants and the bars are packed with
mothers and grandmothers and their broods. Some
restaurants put up their prices for Mothering
Sunday but we think that would bring only short-
term gain and potentially kill our local trade. So we
have our usual Sunday roast lunch menu, plus a
couple of special extras like smoked salmon blinis
especially for the mums.

With Easter just around the corner, there is much
to do this month. Key staff have been on job swops.
This involves the chefs going to work upstairs in
housekeeping, waiters having to do the washing up
and the managers going into the laundry. Now

inter-departmental co-operation and understanding is very high. Lack of understanding of exactly what workmates do can cause friction. Fay in housekeeping was annoyed when one of the chefs implied the women upstairs had it easy and only worked part-time. Now, having spent a day bending over making beds, clearing up other people's mess and shifting furniture, none of the chefs thinks there is anything part-time or easy about working in housekeeping. While it brings greater understanding, it can also solve the problem that Fay is an ardent Manchester United fan and the boys in the kitchen are Southampton supporters.

The new risk assessment study has been done on all dangerous equipment such as the hot roller iron in the laundry. Health and Safety is a major worry for small businesses and we need to be meticulous about keeping up precautions to avoid accidents, as well as being informed and aware of possible danger areas. Sarah, Leon's fiancée, is currently on a government training scheme called a modern apprenticeship. It's an excellent way for young people to gain nationally accredited training qualifications while at work. She has recently attended a special course on Health, Safety and Risk Assessment, and is applying her new knowledge at the hotel, under the guidance of David, who looks after all staff training and appraisals.

The Department of Trade and Industry has chosen us as a case study for best practice and will film interviews with Nick, me and the staff about the minimum wage, working time directive and our positive attitude at the hotel. Our policy on looking after the team that runs the hotel has been used as a role model by a number of organisations, especially the British Hospitality Association. In 1997 the CBI made a video with us, called *Serving Your Best Interests*, which was about having a positive attitude to looking after and training employees. We were also featured in a television business programme called *The Bottom Line*, which looked at how we manage to reduce hours and improve working conditions while we also increase turnover and profit. Everyone we employ is rewarded with good pay and conditions, gifts and benefits, and they are not overworked. This last is a real anomaly in a business noted for its long hours. Our belief that customer satisfaction is a direct result of employee satisfaction has proved a winning combination for many years. It is obvious and simple, and yet apparently many larger organisations find it hard to adopt this attitude. I just don't understand why.

However, the new legislation is a worry and, though we always try to be a good employer, some of the laws proposed in Europe are frightening. Rewards offered as a gift and benefit to employees are now a right. More and more, all sickness or leave of absence has to be met by the employer. This is incredibly costly for the small business. And if unscrupulous workers abuse this right, they can potentially break the small operator, putting him out of business and all the other employees out of a job.

Nick and I take a day off with Pip to go for an open day at Surrey University in Guildford. As we enter, we are separated and given a conducted tour, just like the students. I don't know about Pip but I would love to go and study there. We cast a critical hotelier's eye over the students' accommodation, which is perfect, equipped with every facility and very modern, as is the entire campus. Having accompanied Pip to several universities, I note that this is the first to officially invite the parents, a smart move on their part. As Nick and I work hard to earn the money to pay for our children's university education, we really appreciate the opportunity to see exactly what is on offer should our daughter choose Surrey.

I love learning and wish I could go back to college again too. Part of the training programme we offer at the hotel is based on continuous learning. When, in the early nineties, I returned to college and then on to university to study counselling, the whole experience opened my mind and gave me a clear vision for the business, enabling me to change not only the way I worked but the whole management system at the hotel.

The day after our trip to Guildford I am the main speaker, billed as the Keynote Speaker, at the South West Region's Investors in People Club at the Crown Hotel in Blandford, Dorset. I can hear myself picking up the business jargon as the number of speaking engagements mounts up. I'm talking to representatives from about sixty small and diverse businesses, telling our story – firstly about achieving the business accreditation Investors in People and secondly about the use of the Business Excellence Model and winning the UK Quality Award. This event is a useful rehearsal for a speech I have to give at the British Quality Foundation's main London winners' conference towards the end of the month. As in Cornwall, I expect numbers to be low, but the room looks full and as I sit on the platform listening to the event organiser, I can't believe it is me being introduced. I stand up in front of what proves to be a very friendly and kind audience and hold court. As I explain how we apply the model at the hotel, and our philosophy, my confidence grows. They laugh at all my jokes, or maybe it's the timing – and I can feel they are right with me. For the first time I feel I am working an audience. I finish, get a great applause, and answer questions. I feel enthused and, by the time I leave, I also feel ready for London.

It is the weekend of the Isle of Wight Grand National. For the last two weeks Nick has been up at the course helping Harold George build the series of inviting fences. The local newspaper has featured a picture of them building one of the main jumps, a huge hedge. An amusing advertisement has been broadcast daily on the local radio, encouraging Islanders to come to a day at the races, and the Meridian Television crew are due over early on Sunday morning to film the event. Vets, blacksmiths, doctors, ambulances, stewards of the course and car-parking attendants, programme sales men and women, and jump judges are all being rallied. The Isle of Wight Steam Railway has polished up its trains and will be open to carry families to the course. The ladies' committee, predominantly Isle of Wight Pony Club mums, are organising the food. Not a job I would want. Trying to feed over two thousand people in a field on a cold day in March is not an enviable task. Let's hope it's not cancelled; last year, the event was called off at the last minute and they found themselves left with vast quantities of sausages and hamburgers. At least they don't have to worry about nut allergies and GM foods on their menus. Anthony Goddard, our local brewer (and intrepid skier), is running the beer tent with his delicious Goddard's Bitter. He pulls the pints himself and the thirsty crowds love him. On the evening before the event, Nick and I give a small dinner for one or two of the organisers and main sponsors as a thank you for their support. With plenty of hungry farmers dining, I decide on a menu of fillet of beef served with a rich, full Italian vintage from John Armit Wines. It's a jolly affair and we look forward to an exciting day at the races.

The next morning, the skies have opened and it is pouring with rain. The telephone rings. It's Meridian Television to say they are not coming. My heart sinks when I think of all the people we have hustled and badgered to take part, telling them they would be on the telly. I try to put on a brave face but, to make matters worse, when I arrive at the course the rain has stopped and it's brilliant sunshine. Too late for the television people to reverse the decision but no one understands why they are not there.

Howard Johnson and David Biles are the race commentators. Their entertaining double act is well known and much loved on the Island. These farmers bring each race to life with their droll and clever banter. This year David Biles is High Sheriff of the Isle of Wight and normally arrives at official functions resplendent in his velvet suit and white tights, but today he is proudly standing in the parade ring in his best county tweed suit, topped with a classic brown bowler. When David, a man who loves food and has a fine figure to prove it, first became sheriff, his wife, Diana, had to get him a pair of tights as part of his uniform. Asking at Evans, the outsize shop, for their largest tights, she was assured they were too big for her. 'Oh no,' retorted Diana, 'they're not for me, they're for my husband.'

Young riders on polished fat ponies, looking like something out of Thelwell cartoons, parade the ring for the first event, the Puffing Billy stakes. Anxious mums watch as they fly off over Harold's fences. It's a nail-biting finish, and no fallers. We move on through the day with every race a spectator's dream, local riders, on willing but hardly well-bred racers, battle it out with the slick mainland horses and competitors. Howard, gazing through binoculars, is desperately trying to identify the runners as the horses leap the hedges and swing round the tight bends, spurting on to the finish. Every time a local takes the lead the crowd roars –

Island heroes are much appreciated. The day passes without any problems and I am delighted all horses and riders return home safely. Exhausted, I get back to the hotel, sure that meeting Princess Anne at next week's conference has to be a piece of cake after today. Perhaps I can persuade her to come on the steam train next year.

For the last two weeks I have had telephone calls, emails, faxes and letters confirming details of, and requesting copies of, my presentation at the Winning Through Excellence conference on 25th March. In spite of our recent rehearsals and test runs, I still don't feel used to public speaking and certainly not confident of making a lengthy prepared speech. It's hardly a skill normally needed by hoteliers. I spend weeks writing and rewriting my words. I'm to stand on a platform in front of a huge audience. The opening keynote address will be given by the Patron of the foundation, HRH The Princess Royal. This will be followed by speeches from the three main winners. I am terrified by the enormity of the task before me.

Nick and I arrive at the Cumberland Hotel in London the day before the conference. Staggering in through the swing doors, laden with boxes of bumph, we find no one there to greet or help us, so we disappear up to our room. We hope our guests are receiving a warmer welcome back at the Seaview. There is a rehearsal, followed by dinner with the presenter and other winners, and then we go to bed early to be fresh for our very important breakfast meeting.

Next day a dozen of us stand formally in a private room waiting for the Princess to arrive before the start. She enters very briskly and chats with much charm, appearing so interested in how we won. I immediately forget every word as I stand glazed, and amazed at the day before us. We move off into the main conference hall.

The President of the BQF introduces Princess Anne, then Malcolm Newing, the winner from BT, starts his speech. I follow him. The short video about the hotel that we used at the awards ceremony in October is played on the huge screen, and is followed by a warm applause. I have eight minutes in which to give my speech. I try to walk confidently up to the podium but feel desperately nervous, in front of a stream of blinding lights. The hotel logo, a sailing yacht, is now projected behind me. I use the yacht logo and sailing metaphors to describe the skills required in running a small hotel business. At rehearsals last night the organisers told me I must not refer to 'tweaking the sails' – it might sound too close to 'fiddling the books'. I make some alterations and off I go: . . . running the Seaview is like sailing . . . working like a highly trained racing team . . . tweaking the rigging in order to maximise performance . . . we have been blessed with many gentle breezes, which have filled our sails but we have had our stormy and difficult times when we have had to batten down the hatches to survive . . .

Shaky at the start, my voice settles down and by the end I am feeling really buoyant and get a great round of applause. I sit down at the far end of the long stage waiting for Paul Burden, the reporter from the BBC business programme, to ask questions. Looking out into the audience I see the Princess sitting in the centre of the front row. She smiles warmly and I feel reassured.

Interestingly, another hotelier is the European winner of the Small Business Award. Klaus Kobjoll from the Landhotel Schindlerhof in Germany now travels the world giving professional presentations for a serious fee. I sit on the stage and listen to him in awe. Nick, sitting opposite me on the front row, also finds his presentation fascinating and we pick up great ideas. I particularly like the way he describes his business as being like a cake. Every business has the basic sponge, some also have a rich creamy filling, others an elaborate icing, but the top businesses are the ones with the extra cherries and baubles on top. The little unexpected treats and thoughtful touches which make the customer and employee go 'ooh'. One of Klaus's 'oohs' is a free glass of champagne to settle you down as you check in to his hotel. Another is the daily paper provided for men to read while standing – get this – at the gents' urinal. The speeches and the day roll on, and late that afternoon Paul Burden sums up key points, after which we pack up and leave. Nick and I, exhausted but envigorated, return to the Island.

Once back at the hotel there is no time to stop. Easter is hopping at us. There is a definite shifting up a gear as we approach the holidays. Over 50 per cent of the homes in Seaview village are holiday cottages, many closed up tight for the winter. As the school term ends, mums in four-wheel-drive or estate cars packed with pillows, food, small boats, bicycles, children and dogs, plus all their essentials, arrive to set up home for another year. The village streets, deserted all winter, are crowded with unloading cars. Small children, in jellybean shoes, laden with buckets and crabbing nets, rush down to the still chilly sea. Late on Friday evenings, tired fathers appear, fresh off the ferries or hovercraft, ready to sort out the life jackets and help prepare dinghies for another summer bobbing about in boats. Reluctantly they return to the mainland on Sunday.

The bars are getting busier and many of the bedrooms need extra cots for the children. A week before Easter, we check all the staffing rotas for the bank holiday weekend. Lee the head barman reviews the drinks prices as the main breweries often increase their charges before the season starts. During the winter we run on minimum stock but we need to ensure we don't run out of anything, from Famous Grouse Scotch whisky to sparkling mineral water, over the bank holiday. Procedures that are sometimes not followed precisely to drill during the quieter months have to be sharpened up as we get busier. Guests' names must be clearly marked on all food orders, numbered discs have to be given to people dining on the tables outside so they can be easily identified. New linen, blankets, towels, bathrobes and uniforms have all been bought, along with extra cups, plates, glasses and cutlery.

Then there are the Seaview extras that we always do, like the tiny blue, pink and white speckled chocolate eggs we give with coffee instead of mints during the Easter break. Have we got enough? The chocoholics (especially me) are prone to pinching them. Charlie and his team create new specials to add to the menus daily over the holiday. With the change in clientele there are more adventurous dishes. We buy in some very expensive fresh scollops and serve them lightly seared with fresh ginger and samphire. We begin to be asked for lobster but until the sea calms down the fishermen find it hard to put out their pots and the price is prohibitive.

When we suddenly remember that the clocks spring forward this weekend, there is even less time. We inform all our guests and employees in advance and again on the night. In years past we have had embarrassing incidents after time changes, with plenty of staff but no guests at breakfast or all the guests but no staff. Now we gently remind everyone to get up an hour earlier.

Spring is in the air elsewhere in the hotel. Mark the breakfast chef has fallen in love with Amanda, a pretty Spanish student who is working with us while learning to speak English. Now Amanda is returning to Spain and taking Mark with her just before the busy season starts. Delighted as we are for them, it is a serious problem for the hotel. Rarely have the hotel's many romances, several marriages and even births resulted in someone leaving. In Mark's case, it's particularly sad for us. He came seven years ago to work on the wash-up; after two years, the position of breakfast chef came free and Mark jumped in. He was brilliant. Guests' comment forms came back week after week, month after month, praising his delicious breakfasts. Mark had found his niche and his confidence grew. He's good with eggs. Poached, fried, scrambled, boiled, soft, hard, turned, runny, he can do just what the guests want. Now we urgently need to find and train a replacement before we get too busy. The job advertisement is placed in the local paper. Amanda, now with nearly perfect English, looks radiant and serves breakfast in a very short black skirt. All the men understand why Mark is moving to Spain.

The purchase of Myrtle Cottage is proving difficult. We had hoped for a quick sale in February when we first heard our offer had been accepted, so we could have the place ready for guests this summer. We are told we will need planning permission for the change of use from residential to business premises. The planning application will take weeks. I try not to get too frustrated and keep popping in to the cottage to plan where we will put the beds, what to do with the bathroom and what colours I will paint the walls. I have been wandering around shops choosing items I think will look good when we eventually get the cottage, but can't buy anything yet, just in case our application fails. I've picked out the wall lights, bathroom fittings and kitchen equipment, carpets and curtains, and all before we exchange contracts. It had better work out – Myrtle is already let for the Millennium.

The hotel is full for the end-of-century celebrations. We decide not to be grand but know we
need to plan carefully. The same guests return each
year to celebrate New Year at the Seaview and
many had already booked. We want everyone to
have a special evening but plan not to increase our
normal prices. That way we feel we can please our
regulars, while not overworking our employees. All
those who work during the hotel's four-day
Millennium break are on a profit-sharing scheme
and will benefit directly from their hard work and
the takings generated. Leon and Sarah will be away,
so Nick and I will be very busy managing. We are
not joining in the profit-sharing, but of course we
want to make sure it all runs smoothly.

We start ordering early. We have decided to put
half-bottles of champagne in the guests' rooms
when the beds are turned down in the evening, to
make a surprise when they return after dinner. We
are also looking at individual hand-painted plates
with a simple naive pattern of lobster pots and
crabs, dinghies and rocks, celebrating the fact that
in 2000 we will have owned the Seaview for twenty
years. At every staff meeting we all think up more
ideas and add to the wish list and with nine months
to go we have already ordered the party poppers.
But this week we are more concerned with the final
checklist for Easter.

CHAPTER 7

April
Easter and Europe

Thursday, 1st April, and the Easter break begins –
one of our busiest weekends of the year. The village
has been filling up for days and now the hotel's
weekend guests arrive. Seaview suddenly explodes
with new life. I think back to our first Easter. Ben
was a two-year-old and Pip a baby of six weeks. The
four of us and a tabby cat called Salty lived in a
small flat at the top of the hotel. I had been cooking
for over six months but was still very green. Daily I
negotiated with the local fishermen and farm
suppliers, selected fresh ingredients, changed the
menus, prepared the food and cooked breakfast,
lunch and dinner. I was assisted by Peggy West, a
competent and hard-working grandmother (though
only in her early forties herself), sister of the builder
Willie Caws. Peggy kept me going that first year in
the kitchen. When I was exhausted she would take
over, producing a mug of tea to perk me up; when
I was particularly stressed she appeared with a large
gin and tonic. Easter was my introduction to
cooking in a commercial kitchen under real
pressure with never-ending food orders and
demands. The restaurant was full, the bars were
full, the order board in the kitchen was full and I

was full of terror. It was hard. But somehow, in spite of regularly dashing upstairs, leaving Peggy to hold the fort while I fed Pip, the dishes were cooked and everyone was happy.

I was exhausted that Easter, and we had special extended licensing hours in the bars so we stayed open late. Each night after closing time we poured the last of the locals out the door, and then had to clean up all the mess before we went to bed. Only a few hours more and guests would come down for breakfast. I have never done so much washing up in my life – plates, pots and pans in the kitchen and then all the glasses in the bars. Finally we finished and climbed upstairs to our flat for desperately needed sleep. On the Saturday night the clocks went back so we lost an hour and Pip needed feeding. I wondered why I had ever wanted to go into the hotel business. But at the end of the bank holiday weekend we proudly drove to the bank laden with the generous takings. It was better than we could possibly have imagined.

Over the years we improved, learning to organise more staff for this weekend, especially on the wash-up. With experience we also ordered in larger stocks of everything from lobsters to local bitter. We learned to get in more small change for the bar tills – since the banks would be shut we had to be fully supplied, like a ship at sea. Scrabbling round the local amusement arcades on Easter Sunday, begging for ten- and fifty-pence coins, had been no fun. We learned to take an afternoon nap, as eight hours' sleep was never an option, even without the clocks going back.

After the long hard winters, we began to look forward to Easter and realised it would improve our bank balance. In 1981 we took on a young man called Sebastian Snow. His father was an explorer and his mother an elegant and vivacious Italian. Sebastian arrived fresh from public school unable to boil an egg, but with an inherited Mediterranean love and natural understanding of food and his father's intrepid ability to keep going. He, like us, worked long hours and learned quickly, helping us to survive and find success in our early years. He and Peggy ensured that the meals kept coming out even if I had to rush off to sort out an infant. Now Sebastian owns his own very successful restaurant in London called Snow on the Green.

Julia was born in 1983. I was only just pregnant at Easter but in August I was eight months pregnant and cooked for over eighty every night during that Cowes week. Sebastian and Peggy saw me through, along with Ali who joined us in the kitchen in 1982.

With the birth of Julia came a young nanny called Sammy. Sammy was to change our lives. She was seventeen, tall, slim, a natural blonde with a curvaceous bust and gorgeous face. Every man in the village envied Nick and was certain that he alone had done the interviewing. Sammy was unfailingly kind. She scooped up my children and loved them all. While I worked in the kitchen Sammy changed nappies. Just before Julia was born we bought Jasmine Cottage next to the hotel, behind Lloyds bank, so that we could have a separate home and our own garden. Here our children grew up, close to but not consumed by our passions for the hotel. Later we were able to buy the entire Lloyds bank building and spread out, giving each child his or her own room.

Sammy helped Ben through his fussy-eating stage with food she said had come from outer space. Star Wars was the rage, so Sammy coloured the mash potato blue and Ben happily ate his intergalactic mash. She taught Julia to be brave, standing in the sea and throwing her squealing with delight into the surf. I would never have been so bold, holding on nervously to my child in the water, but Sammy was young and confident and gave Julia courage. Julia went on to win regional and national sports events, especially in long jump, and I know it was Sammy's encouragement that enabled her to leap farther and longer. At the same time she helped Pip learn to read and develop a love of poetry and books.

Sammy married Jay, an intelligent young man with a passion for music and old motorbikes. Pip and Jules were bridesmaids. They proudly danced around their beautiful nanny in white cotton dresses with navy blue sashes, and after their marriage Sammy and Jay sped off from the church in a classic old bike with sidecar, her white dress and veil spilling out of the wobbly old vehicle. They went to live on a houseboat on the river at Newport but she continued to look after the children. It was only when she became pregnant and had her own baby, Tim, that she gave up

This Easter the bedrooms and restaurants are, as usual, booked to capacity. The pubs fill up of their own accord. One problem, especially when we are busy, can be the 'no-shows'. In the beginning, we didn't take a deposit on hotel reservations, trusting our guests to let us know well in advance if they were unable to come. We expected them to pay for the unused room if they failed to cancel in time to allow us to relet the accommodation. On August Bank Holiday 1997, the people who made a four-day booking for our two best rooms didn't turn up, and then refused to pay. We could have let the rooms many times over. Not only did we lose hundreds of pounds on the accommodation but we also lost money the guests would have spent in the bars and restaurant. Losses like this can add up to over a thousand pounds. From then on, we realised we had to take a deposit to confirm a reservation. Buying a holiday abroad, or any domestic package, requires payment in full and in advance. Consumers automatically take out holiday insurance. But there are some people who book rooms in hotels, or tables in restaurants, and think they need not turn up and will not be liable for the cost. Since taking deposits we have lessened the problem in the bedrooms, but we seem to have an increasing problem with the restaurant. People phone and reserve a large table, especially on bank holiday weekends or during Cowes Week, and then neither turn up nor have the courtesy to cancel. It's frustrating to think about the loss. We take telephone numbers and ask parties of more than six to phone the day before to confirm their booking but in spite of all these precautions, we still have a couple of key tables not turn up this Easter.

Ben has taken a break from his studies at Bordeaux university to take the Royal Yachting Association Senior Dinghy Instructor's sailing course. Once again, this summer he hopes to work teaching sailing at the Seaview Yacht Club. We encourage our children to have holiday jobs but don't pressurise them to work in the hotel. Ben started working at the yacht club five years ago, and qualified as a basic instructor a year later. Last summer he left Seaview to work for the Portsmouth-based sailing holiday company Sunsail, at their sailing centre in Greece. Now with a higher qualification and his experience abroad, he hopes to gain a more responsible position with better pay. Young sailing instructors in Seaview are like ski instructors in Val d'Isère. An envied class of males, much admired by the females, they swan around the village with tanned bodies, in trendy sunglasses, nonchalantly sporting life jackets, and followed by a trail of adoring youngsters. We all understand why Ben wants the job. Having qualified, he can look forward to a summer bobbing about on the water. Pip, on the other hand, has chosen to work in the hotel bars. Not an easy choice for her. Julia is looking forward to a summer pursuing her two loves – sailing her fast laser dinghy and riding Nick's horse flat out along the beach.

Having passed his instructor's exams with flying colours, Ben returns happily to his student flat and university in Bordeaux. A few weeks later Julia and I take the train down to see how he is coping after being robbed late at night. He telephoned me early the morning after the robbery, very shaken and urgently in need of money, having lost his wallet, cards and cash. I tried desperately through the English and French banking system to transfer money to him, but found it impossible. It takes at least three working days – five with the weekend – for any transaction. In frustration, I selected at random a Bordeaux hotel from the Michelin Guide and telephoned the manager, explaining my predicament and begging, as a fellow hotelier, for his help. Within an hour money was deducted from my credit card and Ben was able to eat that weekend. As the management of the Hotel Burdigala was so helpful and supportive to us in our need, Jules and I decide to visit Bordeaux and stay there while we see Ben and check out his student digs. We travel down to Paris by Eurostar and then on to Bordeaux by TGV express. It's a comfortable, painless journey with lots of girlie chats. Because of the long hours and seven-days-a-week nature of our business, quality time with the children is very important to me. Tall and athletic, Jules looks much older than fifteen, especially now that she is experimenting with make-up. I test her on her English literature work, *Great Expectations*, and we practice our French so we can keep up with Ben.

It is such fun for me to be back in Bordeaux. The last time I was here was over twenty years ago before I left Corney & Barrow. Then I was on a tasting course with Peter Sichel of Sichel Wines, owner of Château Palmer and Château d'Angludet. While there I was privileged one day to taste every vintage of the wine of Château Palmer from 1961 to 1971 – what a menu for a wine buff. I studied for years with the Wine and Spirit Education Trust and Corney and Barrow, learning how to taste wines and recognise the difference between one vintage and another in Bordeaux. But it was only then, when I stood in that famous château, that my years of training suddenly crystallised in my mind. It was important, working in the wine trade, to know and recognise different vintages, so it was an education in itself to be able to taste this château's wine over ten different years and compare, and take detailed notes on, every aspect of the ten vintages. I could clearly see the subtle differences caused by the countless variables in any given year: how much it had rained that year, whether there had been a long hot summer or a cold wet spring, whether they had picked early or late. Fascinating.

During that last visit I had also been able to taste another very interesting selection of claret. The predominant grape varieties used in making red wine in Bordeaux are Cabernet Sauvignon, Cabernet Franc, and Merlot. In 1970 Château Les Ormes made a wine with only Cabernet Sauvignon grapes, another with only Cabernet Franc, a third with only Merlot grapes, and finally their normal wine with a carefully balanced selection from all three grape varieties. Now we were able to taste each of these red wines and see which of the different grape varieties matured early, which was still full of tannin, and what had happened to the colour. I had returned to London full of confidence and a real understanding of the wines of Bordeaux, along with a certificate from its university. Now here I am, twenty years later, back in the city. It is such fun to go out to dinner with Ben and Jules and introduce them to the different grape varieties and wines, passing on as much of my own knowledge as I can.

On returning to Seaview I am met with a court summons. On the front patio outside the hotel we have a number of ground-level lights. Some are hidden in the flower beds, others light up the path leading to the front door of the hotel. On a warm summer's evening last August, a woman complained she did not like the low lights shining up her skirt, so she had covered the nearby one with her plastic handbag, which had then melted.

When I heard about the incident, I dismissed it as I suggested she could easily have moved away from the light to avoid it annoying her and explained that we had hundreds, if not thousands, of lights in the hotel and covering any of them with a plastic handbag would cause it to melt. Finally, for my own peace of mind I contacted both our electricians and the manufacturers to ensure that the light fittings fully met the approved safety standards. They did.

I thought that was the end of the matter. Now, nine months later, Nick and I are sent a summons. We freeze with fear. It is such a worry in business today. Any legal action, even when you are in the right, costs serious money. Even if we simply replace the plastic handbag, we have no idea of the legal implications of liability and the repercussions, as that could be seen as an acceptance of guilt. If a guest asks us for an aspirin we are not allowed to give it, as we could be sued should the aspirin then have a detrimental effect. It would be giving medical aid. Heavy hearted we contact our solicitor and our insurance company and reluctantly hand the entire affair over to them. Since 1980, with the exception of purchasing property, we rarely use a solicitor. We now find ourselves having almost weekly meetings with Tony Holmes of Roach Pittis over problems on the purchase of Myrtle Cottage, the new employment contracts needed for the Working Time Directive, and now this melting handbag saga.

The English Tourist Board inspector arrives. We normally receive two inspections a year, one from the AA hotel division and one from the RAC. Over the last two years we haven't seen or heard from the RAC, except when they notify us that their fees have doubled, so we decide to stop using them and move over to the ETB. Having sat on the government tourism advisory forum with both the Conservative and Labour governments, I have watched the development of the new harmonisation scheme. This has been designed to simplify the way accommodation is graded, so that the general public can understand the system and not get confused with roses, crowns, stars, rosettes and – on the Isle of Wight – sea horses. Now we just have stars. The Seaview is a three-star hotel. It can't achieve a higher rate of four or five stars because we're a small hotel in a building of limited size and facilities. We don't have or need a swimming pool, sauna, coffee shop or lift. The luxury lies in our personal service and comfort. However, within the three-star criteria we have many rooms that are of four- or five-star standard and a restaurant that has won numerous awards and rosettes. When the inspector arrives, we listen with interest to what he says about each of our rooms and their facilities and we watch out for areas where we can improve. We pay several hundred pounds for this unbiased inspection and value all comments.

One aspect of modern living that the inspector points out is the rise in the use of laptop computers in hotel bedrooms. Business people need to work, so we note that when we redecorate our rooms we must supply not only a hair dryer and elecric point near the mirror, and a shaver point by the sink, but also a socket and phone point near a desk to enable laptops and fax/email modems to be connected. Meanwhile, we temporarily solve the problem by investing in extension leads and small portable desks. The other two Business Excellence Award winners, BT and Nortel, are currently jointly developing a new hotel telephone system. We hope that this will fulfil the latest business requirements as our old BT switchboard cannot monitor the length of calls made on computers. There is talk of us, the third winner, trying out the new system which will, we hope, be good for our business customers to enable us to charge them correctly to guests' bills. The inspector is very upbeat about the hotel and thoroughly approves of our operation. He notices and values the excellent service provided by all our employees but he also points out that the old building is quite restricting. Two small single rooms only have showers, no baths, and that counts against us.

The Isle of Wight Council is hosting a visiting group of councillors from Ostholstein, a town in northern Germany. They have booked nearly all the hotel accommodation and want us to lay on our best service and do everything in our power to impress these guests. So we roll out the red carpet. Interestingly, the German councillors are high-profile business men and women or professional academics, whereas over here those in business or the professions are often too busy to get involved in local politics. The Germans love the Island, especially our village. They return to Germany laden with gifts including Isle of Wight glass, and a clear and positive view of the Island, having dined on fresh local crab in our hot crab ramekin and Adgestone wine from the Arreton valley in the centre of the island.

The increased business this year has been good for our budgets and targets as we approach the end of our financial year. Nick and I have a simple budget system. We compare our figures week on week, month on month and year on year, looking for approximately a ten-per-cent annual increase, depending on inflation. We compare our weekly takings against our highest cost, labour, and if the percentage of wages against turnover goes up we know we need to look at how many staff are on duty and if they are all needed. If the business increases but we manage to keep the labour costs down, the hotel is doing well. This is only a simple and rough guide but it seems work.

Our accounting year end is 30th April so we begin to think about the budget for next year. With computer systems and new technology it is so easy to churn out all sorts of facts and figures about the business, but it is never simple. Our accountant is arranging for us to have not only a more sophisticated budget breakdown but quarterly accounts too. I am sure it is all very interesting but the Luddite in me thinks the old system works well and wonders why we need to increase our stress and paperwork, complicating the way we assess our success by more accounts. Nick is much more a figures person than me and so decides the new accounts will help. He and our accountant Andrew Porteus work on. One reason I like to keep things simple is because if they get too complicated, I no longer understand what's important. In addition, we share our information with all our employees and must present facts so that they can be easily absorbed by a wide range of staff.

Nick and I work in a business partnership. We are not a limited company. When we started this was sensible, and even though the business has expanded dramatically over the years we have still not formed a limited company. One danger of the partnership is that if things go wrong we would lose everything: our business, our house, the whole lot. At times this can be very frightening and even though we both know the hotel constantly improves and grows, this fear has been a healthy driving force in keeping us progressing forward.

Though we took on serious borrowings at the beginning, we have always kept within our means and flourished as a result. We frequently have had to wait both to make improvements and to take on further investments, and this slow and steady growth has been good for us and the business. For example, we were not able to invest immediately in all the private bathrooms, but had to build them one at a time. With every addition I learned a great deal, and consequently each room is unique. Every aspect of the development of the hotel has been an interesting learning experience, though some have also been frustrating.

Recently we have been debating about how to shut out the light from the opaque glass roof in the Sunshine Restaurant. Though the glass makes the room very light and airy it is unwanted when companies use the room to give demonstrations and presentations. It can also get very hot in the summer. We need to fit special blinds, but I can't find anything to fit in with the décor. The entire restaurant is themed on boats, with the floor in pale decking, the stainless-steel yacht shrouds protecting the large model of a French destroyer, the ship's grab rail round the edge of the room and the antique ships' models and wooden half models from Larry Longford's beautiful model shop on the King's Road in London.

As spring progresses we need more help in the bars. An advertisement is placed, not for a barman or barmaid but a 'bar person'. Nick has learned from the solicitor that we need to be scrupulous about avoiding any instances of sex discrimination. Everyone is warned to be careful when talking to new applicants on the phone. We study the wording on our job applications and now keep the details of anyone who fills in an application form, even if they are not suitable, for over a year, in case they put in a claim. All we want is some extra help in the bars. The interviews start, we all know what kind of person we are looking for, but he or she is not easy to find. Few respond to the advertisement in spite of its appearing in the local paper for two weeks. Some who complete the application form then don't wish to be interviewed. Those who make it through the interview stage are invited in for a trial run. Two applicants make it through the interview, and one doesn't turn up for the trial. The other, having done the trial and accepted the job, then doesn't turn up for work. Recruiting staff is difficult, time-consuming and frustrating. Finally we find James. He is perfect, seems to fit in and we are all delighted as he will join the team next month. Dilemma solved, I hope.

Another visit is due, this time from the assessors in charge of the Investors in People scheme. One of the main reasons why we started to try to achieve IIP accreditation was because we realised it formalised the hotel's policy to all its employees. We started with an initiative through our local DTI-sponsored Business Link called Partners in Success, and then progressed on to achieve IIP. One of the benefits of this award is a reduction in staff turnover. We knew that reducing the number of staff who leave meant we would not waste time constantly trying to recruit new people. After gaining the national accreditation some years ago, this month we are now being reassessed. For years Nick and I had our business plan in our head. Then, as the number of our employees grew, we formalised what we were doing and how we were going to do it. IIP encouraged us to have a clearer business plan, along with a detailed policy on staff education and training. We wrote down for the first time our vision, to have 'The perfect small seaside hotel run by a happy team dedicated to the art of delighting our guests'. This now appears on the bottom of the minutes of every staff meeting.

We always invested heavily in training, but we haven't always kept detailed records, not only of who went on which course, but more particularly monitoring the benefits overall from training each year. Now, from the moment someone answers an advertisement we try to make their experience of the hotel pleasant and useful. We take a great deal of time and trouble to show them round the business. If they accept the position, they are given a full induction by our manager, David. All the other staff are notified of the name of their new colleague, who is given a friendly welcome into the hotel. Shortly after they begin, new members of staff are given an appraisal so they can see where they are going and where they may need further training. We send every member of staff on at least one course per year, but we have ongoing in-house training every day at the hotel. They have a detailed job description of the areas they are to cover and all new employees are trained by a colleague for at least a week at the beginning before they work on their own.

Dan has taken over Mark's job as breakfast chef and, while everyone encourages him, we also have to ensure that the quality of the breakfast he is producing is up to the high standard of his predecessor. After only a few weeks Dan is doing well, but Philippa, worried that his poached eggs are not quite right yet, is keeping a close eye on his progress. The assessor interviews over half our workforce to ensure that we continue to follow all the correct procedures.

There is an unconfirmed report of a rat near the rubbish area at the far end of the hotel car park. We call in the council pest control immediately. When we bought the Seaview we discovered cockroaches in a back store. Infestation is all part of the darker side of the food industry. Every place gets hit with it, like head lice in young children. Since that day we have had contractors (most recently a local firm called Hillbans) regularly check the entire hotel upstairs and below stairs for any unwanted pests. We can check the inside of the property daily, but we need professional help to get into the less accessible corners, outside stores and particularly the rubbish areas, which can attract everything from large bluebottle flies to our most recent unwanted, whip-tailed visitor.

The pest control inspectors are expensive but vital. They safeguard us and our guests, shining their bright torch into every dark corner to ensure the hotel is safe. Every window in the kitchen is covered with a washable fly screen and a large fluorescent exterminator dispenses with any insect that enters the *cordon sanitaire* with a spark of crackling efficiency. The Hillbans pest controller assures us that there is no evidence of a problem, but we all agree to increase surveillance for a couple of weeks to make sure. By way of an added precaution I regularly walk Millie out through the car park. Though no official rat catcher, she would be delighted to dispose of any unwanted intruders on her territory.

Charlie and Tom are going up to London with me for the day. We are visiting the fish department at the head office of Marks and Spencer. A good friend, Lou Bland, has been working in the food section of M & S for a number of years. She keeps in touch with current food trends, has a close liaison with top chefs and restaurants, and is very much at the cutting edge of creating innovative new dishes which are not complicated to prepare. I have known Lou, daughter of our friend Christopher

Bland, for years and watched her progress from talented chef to high-powered business woman. She has kindly arranged for us to look round the department and observe how M & S develop their fish products. We meet other members of the team, see how they place orders, source the freshest supplies of fish from all over the world and deliver them to their customers. It makes our tiny operation at the Seaview look so simple, yet procuring the best quality fresh products is never an easy task.

As the supermarkets now retail such sophisticated food products, particularly in their prepared meals, they are now in competition with restaurants. I thought it would be useful for our chefs to see how M & S developed their meals. Once we had a delicious starter with tomato, aubergine and mozzarella cheese on our menu. A week after we put it on the menu M & S had a very similar dish in their prepared meal section. Consumers may buy-in a prepared dinner rather than go to a restaurant, so we need to be different at the Seaview. We are up in London putting our heads together to gain inspiration from the way M & S research and develop their dishes. We join in an exercise in quality control, looking at every aspect of appearance, smell, flavour and taste. It's just like wine tasting, really. Then we visit a number of the different departments including the one that designs the packaging and another buying in all the raw fish. We compare notes on current food trends and problems and leave feeling most grateful for the insight into such a huge, quality operation.

After the visit to Marks and Spencer we go to lunch at Antony Worrall Thompson's latest restaurant, Wiz. There we try a range of inter-nationally accented dishes. We look at classic English food, Mediterranean, and Far Eastern flavours. We analyse each dish, picking up on a white bean crush with fresh rosemary and also on their delicious English fishcakes. Before leaving London we pop into the Conran Shop in Fulham Road to see how Terence Conran's designer look in the home has developed into his huge new-wave restaurants, seating four to five hundred. Last year, when we had lunch at his restaurant Quaglino's, we were also treated to a tour of the kitchen with the head chef. Now, wandering round the beautiful hand-made, slick, modern furniture at Conran's, it is easy for the chefs to see how its owner moved on to modern designer food, set in sleek and efficient new restaurants that treat the diner to a totally modern experience. He has changed the world's perception of the old English restaurant. London is now the place to go to experience great modern food, just as much as Paris or New York. We drive back full of enthusiasm and before we arrive at the ferry terminal at Portsmouth we have planned the next set of menus.

CHAPTER 8

May
Mayday and Mermaids

May begins with the first of two bank holidays. So the month starts with a bang. As the temperature rises, so does the pressure. May Day, introduced by the Labour government in the seventies, is normally the quietest holiday. This year is different. People are taking a lot of notice of the Seaview. Not only that, but short breaks in England are increasingly popular. We are exceptionally busy. I take the orders in the restaurants on Saturday night. We have over eighty booked and though we endeavour to stagger reservation times, everybody seems to arrive at once. At the same time both the bars and tables outside fill with people wanting bar snacks.

Though Nick appears cool and calm, I know he is tense. He checks the restaurants, reassuring himself there are adequate supplies of chilled mineral water, red and white wine, butter, sugar, sweeteners, cream, after-dinner mints, cutlery, china, glasses, coffee, napkins, tablecloths and baskets of freshly baked bread and crusty rolls. He wanders round looking at each place setting, moving a fork, glass or cruet into line. He is preparing for combat. I check that the flowers have plenty of water and that all the staff are looking clean and smart and know their parts. Though we don't have a formal uniform as such, everyone wears black and white. Occasionally new members of staff appear in brown shoes or unpressed shirts which will not do and they have to be gently encouraged to smarten up. At the moment, because it is warm the boys are asking if they can shed the black waistcoats while working behind the bar and in the restaurant.

At eight o'clock most of the tables are still empty and I have taken only three orders. By eight thirty nearly everyone is sitting down and the bars are surging with people wanting to give food orders. It is impossible for the kitchen. I quickly take half a dozen restaurant orders, then wander round chatting to the other guests, telling them anecdotes, and encouraging them to have a first or second aperitif before I take their order, so as to spread out the rush in the kitchen. The chefs can prepare only a certain number of dishes in one go, up to about ten, and until one bunch goes out to the customers, the kitchen can't start the next batch.

At each table I fill in a restaurant docket. One copy for the chefs and a second to stay in the restaurant and later to be used by the office to make up the bill when required. It is important to write clearly, putting down the customer's name, the number of diners in the party, the date, the time the order is taken and the table number. Nick, Leon, David and I, together with the reception staff, always carry a list of that evening's guests. We check we know the names before service, but sometimes a familiar face arrives and I just can't remember their name. It's embarrassing, but I normally manage to bluff my way through without having to refer to the list. Nick is amazing. He always remembers everyone. He even keeps a little reminder book with details – for example, the actor Peter McEnery is recorded as Steam Train Actor because he has his own private miniature train on a track in his garden and is a real steam buff. Sometimes guests are recorded according to their shape and size, others are found under their friends or associates, one by the colour of his rather glamorous speed boat.

When I take orders I sometimes offer help or an explanation of the ingredients and how the dish is prepared. If it is local fish or lobster I can even say where it was caught. Occasionally I get carried away with a story and Leon or Nick have to remind me that there are another seventy-five orders to go. At other times the chefs are overloaded and want me to stop orders for a moment so they can catch up.

As the evening progresses everyone seems delighted with their meal. They are oblivious to the heat and the pressure building up in the kitchen before their meals are collected by the dining-room staff and taken into the restaurant. The chefs, now very hot and tired, actually finish quite early at about 10.30pm, having scrubbed down their solid-top range and swept and washed their area of floor. But I'm glad I haven't been doing the cooking on this busy night.

Sunday proves even harder. The restaurants

normally close on Sunday night because most weekend guests have gone home, and we serve meals in the bars, unless a guest particularly wants to sit in the restaurant. However, over a bank holiday the residents stay until Monday, so we keep all the restaurants open on Sunday. This year, when we have cleared away after serving thirty-six roast Sunday lunches and numerous bar snacks, we start to prepare for the seventy booked that evening in the restaurant. Vacuum-cleaners are out, table-cloths and linen napkins are washed and ironed, plates, glasses and cutlery are polished and stocks of everything are once again replenished. To add to our problems, we are short-staffed and everyone begins to feel tired as the weekend progresses. On a normal Sunday night, with the restaurants shut, the managers – including Leon, David, Charlie and Nick – are able to have the night off. But not this weekend. The diners arrive and Nick is taking the orders. Unfortunately, just as on the previous night, everyone packs in at once. Nick tries to keep all the guests happy, and instead of staggering the dockets' arrival in the kitchen, starts taking all the orders at once. Then Leon and David follow his example. The kitchen staff are inundated and have to shout 'STOP!' Because the weather has been good, all the tables in the bars are packed and many others are dining outside. It is a very hectic night. Monday morning, and we are exhausted.

Every year the Seaview Residents and Business Association organises a May Fair. On Monday the High Street, fringed in bunting, is closed to cars early in the morning and enthusiastic volunteers grab their pitches and set up stalls. The Royal National Lifeboat Institute table is full of RNLI merchandise, pens and calendars, napkins and tea towels. Next door Mr and Mrs Fox-Basset are selling charming hand-made pale-yellow-and-navy-blue wooden wastepaper bins decorated with nautical scenes in aid of the Earl Mountbatten Hospice. There are tables filled with pots of young geraniums and busy lizzies, Victoria and coffee sponge cakes, pots of home-made raspberry jams, marmalade and green tomato relishes. Nick and I wander up past the raffle stall that includes the hotel's prize of a magnum of Corney & Barrow wine and buy three of the jolly wastepaper bins. As I look at the home-made jams and cakes, I wonder how long it will be until EU regulations stop the production of these delicious products. We chat to all the hard-working and enthusiastic participants and return to our own work at the hotel. The fair brings many Islanders into the village. The sun is still shining and the atmosphere continues to buzz as customers arrive at the hotel for a light lunch before our visitors set off back to the mainland. The tired staff put on a brave face and quicken their step to ensure a fast and efficient service. The first May bank holiday is definitely not quiet this year.

During a day trip to London I return to Corney & Barrow's wine bar at 109 Old Broad Street in the City. Their former headquarters – squashed into a tiny office block, decked in wood, with an internal lift to bring up supplies from the bars below – has gone and is replaced by a completely new modern complex. When I started with the firm in 1973, a huge building was being constructed on the opposite side of the road, its foundations dug deep into the site of the original C & B cellars. During the years when I worked in Old Broad Street, the structure rose up to dwarf the entire area. It was the NatWest tower. Today many of the surrounding buildings have been modernised, or, like 109, completely rebuilt.

I wander into the heavily glazed, informal wine bar, now run predominantly by women casually dressed in pale mauve polo shirts and trousers. Smart professional barmen in black bow ties no longer mix Bloody Marys to help City gents through the morning or serve glasses of rich Malmsey after lunch accompanied by a slice of home-made Madeira cake. Now it is Chardonnay and bottles of Beck's beer. I introduce myself at the bar, but the manager is busy in a staff meeting so I order a drink, sit down and look around at the clean designs, pinpoint lighting, expanse of glass, stainless-steel fittings and row upon row of gleaming wine bottles plastered with modern labels. It is very different from the smokey club atmosphere of the once all-male institution, with its dark mahogany panelled walls and classic long bars. Since I left in 1980, Corney & Barrow restaurants have grown from the two bars at Old Broad Street and London Wall to the chain of twelve highly successful and fashionable wine bars and restaurants which are now in operation all over London. I leaf through the company in-house glossy magazine, with its royal warrant and emblems of over two hundred years in the wine trade, but also stamped with modern business logos that include Investors in People. Later I have a conducted tour with Sophie the young, energetic manager and marvel at how far C & B have advanced since their foundation in 1780.

Back home, the yachting season is getting under way in Seaview. The name Seaview is now one word but the yacht club still uses two: Sea View. Towards the end of the last century there was a telegraph office in a house called Neptune, on the seafront, next to the club. Telegraph messages were charged by the number of words, so the canny locals, in the interests of economy, joined up the village name. The hotel took the same title as the village, but the yacht club, whose members were more affluent, stuck to the two words.

Early in May the fleet of Sea View Mermaids returns. These pretty yachts, owned and maintained by the club, are a one-design, twenty-six-foot keelboat. Now they go back into the water, having been stored and repaired during the winter at Coombes yard in Bembridge. The club then bring them round the coast from the shelter of the harbour to their summer moorings, in the sea on an exposed easterly point just off Quay Rocks, clearly visible at the foot of the high street. Each one has a different coloured hull with matching spinnaker.

The brilliant white sails and elegant outline are a familiar summer sight, as helmsmen jostle for position at the start of each race, and red, yellow, blue and green spinnakers billow out as they sail on what is known as a run, towards the buoys. From late spring to early autumn, Nick races the boats on Wednesday and Thursday evenings. At the beginning of the season everyone is rusty but full of enthusiasm. At about 5.30 pm on race nights he sets off with his crew, normally Anthony Goddard. By 5.45 the club nanny boat taxis them, along with all the other boat crews, out to the Mermaids and everyone climbs aboard and is busy rigging the yachts and preparing to let go of the mooring. Then bang, they get a ten-minute gun, so they can start timing how long they have before the start of the race. There follows a five-minute gun and then finally the off. For approximately an hour and a half they tack and jibe round a course set by the race officers in the club, returning to the bar for a pint of Anthony's brew to discuss tactics and weather conditions. For Nick it is a great way to relax, away from the constant demands of the hotel. It is also a huge contrast to the crowded Tube journey we had to take at the same time when living in London. With the wind on his face Nick is glad he left the city.

During the day the Mermaids are chartered for training purposes by large corporations or the armed forces. Yacht racing is an excellent way to develop team-building skills. There is hardly a day when the boats are not booked. This corporate business early in the season is also good for the hotel. Some of the larger houses in the village offer B&B to the visiting yachtsmen and across the street the Northbank Hotel opens in the spring and closes in the autumn when the boats return to Bembridge. This week Marley Tiles, a company that has been racing at the club since before we bought the hotel, has once again brought their sailing teams over and they are staying with us and at the Northbank. They arrive in the village on Thursday night and meet up in the hotel bars or dine in the restaurant. The next morning, after an early breakfast, they enjoy an exciting day's racing and return to a formal dinner and presentation at the yacht club.

The following week a major computer company, ICL, brings a delegation to Seaview for lunch at the hotel, followed by a talk from Nick on how we use the Business Excellence model and won the award. This is ICL's first visit to the Island and Nick's first presentation on home ground. He spends days ensuring his speech is informative and well rehearsed. Talking to representatives from a global corporation about business is still very strange for us. By the time they leave, they are full of ideas for future training sessions chartering the yacht club Mermaids; and they know the hotel's award-winning approach.

We have been invited to a party in London to celebrate twenty-five years of *Holiday Which?* When I joined the government tourism forum in 1996, Patricia Yates of *Holiday Which?* was also a member. I admired her well-informed contributions and clear understanding of the industry. She presented intelligent suggestions in an uncomplicated way, without using annoying jargon and doublespeak. Patricia and her family, along with other members of her team, also made regular visits to the hotel, inspecting for the guide. It was therefore delightful to receive an invitation from Patricia to join in their twenty-five-year celebrations. However, while Nick and I are happy in our own restaurant chatting to guests, we both feel rather lost in a big party where we don't know many others. It is good to see Patricia and to help *Which?* celebrate, but we don't stay long.

We are also off to London's latest fashionable venue, the newly refurbished and highly acclaimed restaurant, Sheekey's. I have been before, once many years ago with my father, when it was a fish restaurant famous for pre- and post-theatre dinner, and when I went again a few weeks ago I immediately realised Nick would be fascinated by the clever new regime. It is now owned and run by the same highly professional partnership that, in recent years, made the Caprice and the Ivy restaurants two of London's most chic eating establishments. On our arrival at its premises just off St Martin's Lane, in Covent Garden, we are welcomed by a doorman who respectfully stands aside, and ushers us in. Passing the bar, which is laden with champagne bottles and oysters on ice, we are shown into a small panelled room with black-and-white photographs of old movie stars. We sit down at a slightly protruding table, close to our neighbours and opposite a picture of a young Jack Hawkins. While we wait to order, the manager arrives to apologise because the light above our table is not working. He explains how he spent most of the afternoon trying to get it fixed but without success. We smile sympathetically. We know exactly what he has been going through. We had horrendous problems with exactly the same light fitting in our restaurant.

We chat, and when the manager realises we are in the trade all barriers are down and it is as though we are old familiar colleagues discussing the business. We discover that this competent young man wants to buy his own small business out of London. He believes his life will be less hassled and stressed. We don't disillusion him. In fact, with Nick looking tanned and fit from sailing, the manager wants to move out of the city immediately. We invite him down to Seaview to see what running your own small business is really like. He can discover first-hand that many of his worries, including the light-bulb problem, will dog him even out of town.

He leaves us, shortly to return with complimentary gull's eggs and celery salt. As we glance down at the menu, ignoring the beluga caviar, our eyes alight on jellied eels with Sarsons malt vinegar, Morecambe Bay potted shrimps, Sheekey's fish pie, Cornish fish stew, and (my real favourite) grilled Dover sole. We decide not to have the fillet of sea bass at £21.75. We are so spoilt and privileged on the Island where local fishermen bring in buckets full of huge bass caught just off Seaview. The chefs fillet them and we are able to offer our customers the freshest portions of this delicious fish for only £13.95.

Divided into a series of small rooms, there is nothing modern, slick, noisy or flash about Sheekey's. The sophisticated clientele, though eating in slightly cramped conditions, obviously enjoy the combination of a dignified, old-fashioned atmosphere, the smart classic design, excellent food and the buzz. It is definitely Nick's kind of restaurant.

The quote for the electrical work at Myrtle Cottage arrives. It is over £4,000 before VAT. I telephone Mike Berry of Berry Electrics to explain that, while I appreciate and value the quality of their work and know they are the best on the Island, it is only a two-up-two-down cottage and the heating is gas. We thought it would cost about £2,000. Mike comes round to see where we can make reductions. As a commercial letting unit, there is only so much we can allocate financially before it ceases to be a viable proposition for the hotel. Myrtle Cottage is proving to be very frustrating before we even get in the door. Our winter dreams of additional family accommodation for the hotel are turning into a summer nightmare.

We have had to put off the firm putting in the new damp course three times because of delays in exchanging contracts. There is a further problem with the change of use. The cost of the damp course is also over £4,000 plus VAT and, with all the problems and delays, the solicitor's bills are mounting daily. Even after we take possession and complete the damp work we will have to wait eight weeks for the walls to dry out before we can start the refurbishment. Not only have we missed the main season, but at this rate we are going to be over budget, as I only allowed £20,000 to decorate and kit out the cottage. Nick patiently plods on with the negotiations with the planning office and solicitors and I try to keep enthusiastic, looking at more paint colours, fabrics, cookers and light fittings. Will it or won't it happen?

On 16th May the review of the hotel by David Wickers following his visit in March, appears in the *Sunday Times*. It is brilliant and the phone hasn't stopped ringing. We are thrilled with the way he describes us and especially like this: 'The Seaview is the car equivalent of a hatchback whose modest outside lines conceal a high-performance engine capable of running many of the well-known *grandes marques* into the ground. Step inside what appears to be little more than a conventional seaside guesthouse, and you find not just one of the best hotels on the Isle of Wight, but one of the best seaside addresses in the country.' The Golden Pillow Award, complete with a special *Sunday Times* certificate, arrives. We are proud to have yet another trophy to hang on the wall for visitors to see.

Halfway through May, Nick is off on an all-male cycling trip. Each year he goes away for three or four days with the same group of men to different areas of northern France. This Isle of Wight *Tour de France* is not timing, Lycra and cycling helmets but good hotels, renowned for their cuisine, and huge gourmet picnics washed down with copious amounts of fine wine. Early in their exploits they became known as the Rhino-sore-arse Club – something to do with their bottoms and the bicycle saddles! They claim to cover sixty or more miles a day, but as half of them don't cycle but travel in the support vehicles, and the remainder wobble after the wine washed down at lunch, nobody really believes them. Each year the whole event is recorded for posterity by Brian Palmer with delightful drawings and an amusing verse, though the less said the better about his appalling school-boy jokes at the end of the publication.

Leon and I are left to run the hotel. It is not a problem but the business is never the same without Nick's quiet and assured attention to detail. I feel slightly aggrieved as his first day away is our twenty-second wedding anniversary, but I calm down when I return home after a long morning in the hotel to discover an enormous and stunningly beautiful arrangement of flowers. With the guests, staff and two dogs to look after, I have little time to feel sad and am kept very busy. I joke with one or two of the regular customers, imploring them not to tell Nick if things aren't as good as usual, but to keep it our little secret – otherwise he will only get big-headed. It is, however, always difficult when Nick is away because he is so charming and good at hosting the hotel that customers expect him always to be here.

Nick and his mates are cycling around the Ardennes, along the old Western Front and down to Verdun. They tour round the fields and visit the cemeteries of the First World War. Nick calls up to share this moving experience, but I am concentrating on taking orders and too busy to listen. He returns tired, heavier in spite of all the exercise but mentally refreshed, ready for the second May bank holiday now coming up round the bend.

A couple of days after Nick's return I catch an afternoon ferry and drive up to London with Lou Dorley-Brown, wife of one of the other cyclists. We are off to see Noël Coward's *Private Lives* starring Juliet Stevenson at the National Theatre. We arrive on a sunny spring evening, park and go for a stroll along the southern embankment of the river. We find ourselves staring up at the Oxo Tower, recently converted into one of the South Bank's smartest restaurants. Never off duty, I persuade Lou to pop up with me and have a look.

As we come out of the lift we see the formal restaurant on one side and the brasserie on the other. It isn't even six o'clock yet but the bar is busy with young city traders having a drink after work and the brasserie is over half full with pre-theatre diners. Knowing it is booked up for months I casually enquire about a table. Amazingly, we are in luck. They have a table for two on the terrace outside, overlooking the Thames, but we have to be out by 7.30pm. That's no problem as the play starts then and we need to be in our seats well before. The panoramic view of the city, up and down river, is absorbing. We both stare out, transfixed by all the buildings, old and new: the Tower of London, St Paul's cathedral, the NatWest tower, Charing Cross, the Savoy Hotel and the Houses of Parliament. Immediately below us the fast flowing water is dotted with vessels ploughing up and down, while the opposite bank is lined with floating restaurants and clubs.

Silver-coated menus embossed with the OXO logo arrive, with details of the special quick two-course pre-theatre meal, including a glass of wine, at £13. The food is modern, simple and delicious with a combination of international flavours. Lou has a warm chicken-liver salad, while I try a spicy vegetarian Indian dish with aubergine; Lou follows with chargrilled ostrich steak and I have seared salmon on crushed pulses. The flavours are strong, intense, beautifully balanced and very good. Both restaurant staff and clientele are young and trendy, with spiky hair and mobile phones. Everyone seems highly professional, be they part of the establishment or customers negotiating their latest deal. The sun is low as we finish off our meal with a perfect cappuccino before leaving for the theatre. London feels full of energy and alive, and Lou and I realise we must bring our older children, now in their late teens, to experience this vibrant atmosphere. It is so different to the casual relaxed feel of dining outside the Seaview. It's good to see the contrast.

We enjoy the play, though we find the casting

interesting. Juliet Stevenson towers over her leading man, even in flat ballet pumps. It takes some of the romance out of the performance. During the interval we indulge in an ice cream and marvel at the language and skill of Coward. Unfortunately, the play runs over time and because it's a full house we have to queue to get out. By the time we reach the car it is well past 10.30pm. We rush off towards Putney and the A3 back to Portsmouth. It's seventy miles from London to the ferry and we have just over one hour to do a journey which normally takes nearly two. We are booked on the midnight ferry. If we miss the boat we will not get home until nearly 3am. That's one of the drawbacks to living on an island. I speed down the road, hoping the flashing police cameras do not contain film, and reach Portsmouth in double-quick time, screeching round the town roundabouts on the way to the ferry terminal. We turn the corner into the port on the dot of midnight and I feel sure we have missed the boat. Luckily the Wightlink crew let us on board just before bringing up the ramp. Good on you, mates.

Mike Orchard has started painting the outside of the hotel. It has been far too wet to do it earlier. Being situated near the sea and its eroding salt spray means that we have to constantly repaint, normally about every three to four years. This year Mike has quoted £6,000 plus extras. Most of the front and side of the hotel is natural stone or brick and doesn't need painting, but all the frames, pipes, doors and windows have to be done. The guests probably won't notice the difference but if we leave it the paintwork will soon start to peel and crack. There is one area immediately above the Sunshine Restaurant on the side of the hotel where Mike needs scaffolding. At the same time Caws & Hermans will try to mend a leak which keeps causing damp patches on the restaurant ceiling. Another expense with nothing to show except no damp patch.

Summer approaches and Nick and I realise that we have been working very long hours. We start early each morning at ten past seven and try to have a break in the afternoon before going back to work in the evening. Until recently there has been so much to do that we find it hard to stop and often go on until nearly five, starting again just after six. We decide to discipline ourselves and stop at half past two. No business calls are to be put through to the office in our house from that time, until we come back on duty at night. Sometimes this is not possible and often our only break is when we go riding, sailing or away from the Island. We know that keeping a constant eye on the business is one of the things that makes us good hoteliers, but it can be very draining and destructive too. Even when we do get away we still find ourselves thinking about the business, how we can improve and what we will do next. It's our chosen way of life, but we need some time off.

The month ends as it began, with another busy bank holiday. This one really marks the beginning of summer. At Easter the first of the village holiday homes were opened up after the winter and since then a trickle of families have continued to come down at weekends. But suddenly everyone is here. Pip and Jules are on half term and our house, like the hotel and village, is alive with young voices and the constant ring of teenage friends on the telephone. Pip is about to start her A-levels. Things are tense and we all treat her with kid gloves, trying to be helpful, but she is very worried. She has worked well and we know she will do her best, but she is hard on herself and has very high standards and expectations. I feel for her but there is nothing I can do, and we have all to try to live together in some degree of harmony over the hectic weekend.

Tomatoes and asparagus from the Arreton valley and fresh local lobsters are needed in good supply for the bank holiday. The Island really looks at its best at this time of year. Everything is fresh, lush and green before the start of the main holiday season. All we need for a perfect bank holiday is excellent weather, but the forecast is not hopeful. The louder voices with smarter accents arrive, wanting the best of everything, including sunshine.

These days in Seaview there is an unmistakable atmosphere of affluence, verging on hysteria. Houses in the village, and particularly those facing the sea, are fetching huge prices, double what they were twelve months ago. Everyone wants to buy. The streets are littered with expensive cars, and mobile phones are at the ready on every table in the bar. Everyone is poised to make a deal. Nick and I think that we have seen it all before, in 1989. The

CHAPTER 9

June
British Tomatoes and French Soup

I wake up at 6.45am to hear a discussion on the radio, with John Humphrys talking about Isle of Wight tomatoes. David Agonbar, head of Wight Salads, is drumming up support for British tomatoes on Radio 4's *Today* programme. The Arreton valley, in the centre of the Island, is coated in an expanse of glasshouses, where miles of carefully nurtured tomato vines produce thousands of plum, cherry, beefsteak and classic tomatoes. The Island, with its record for long hours of sunshine, has the perfect climate in which to grow these shiny red fruit.

The British Tomato Growers Association is a powerful lobby, especially among its members on the Isle of Wight. The co-operative includes many companies with the highest standards of business practice. Through the Island's Business Link, Arreton Valley Nurseries and Wight Salads were introduced to the same business consultant that we use: we all achieved IIP the same year and we have all been recently re-accredited. It is so important for any business to work closely with their suppliers and so satisfying when you are both aiming towards the same high standards.

Individual growers on the Island found environ-mentally friendly ways of producing the quality and flavour now demanded by the supermarkets. The labour-intensive fertilising of the tomato plants by crop workers has now been replaced by natural pollination by bumblebees. Not only is this ecologically beneficial but it makes good business sense as the bees don't demand wages or join unions. A second benefit is that bumblebees have to live in a chemically free environment. Avoiding the use of pesticides, the growers use tiny predatory wasps to control the white fly.

Bad publicity about American genetically modi-fied tomatoes has had a devastating effect on the British market. Now David is on national radio with an effective counterblast to banish consumer fears that British tomatoes are GM. The irony, of course, is that not only are they not GM, but they are produced in such a natural environment.

Last week Rick Stein came to film a programme about Isle of Wight tomatoes. Rick, like David, is amusing and good at promoting the attractions, intense tangy flavour and numerous health benefits of the funny-looking red fruit. Since tasting the concentrated flavour of our local produce, he has ordered a supply of Isle of Wight tomatoes to be delivered twice a week to his restaurant in Padstow, Cornwall.

Another aspect of the British tomato growers' promotion is taking place here on the Island. Nick and local councillor Angela Hewitt are official tasters and judges in a competition. Angela, a superb cook, once owned and ran her own restaurant in Newport, the capital of the Island. The pair of them have great fun tasting and trying the different varieties and flavours, and a picture of them, surrounded by tomatoes of all shapes and sizes, appears in this week's issue of our local newspaper. Meanwhile, back at the hotel, Charlie and I are trying out lots of new tomato dishes for our summer menu. We look at various chilled tomato soup recipes. Each year we have gazpacho on the menu for the summer but chilled Island tomato and fennel soup is tasting delicious.

There is a problem locking up the hotel. Last night money was left out and the tills were not reconciled properly. We need to establish where the procedure is going wrong and why. At the end of a shift the staff are tired and all they want to do is get home. Unfortunately, there is a long process to follow before they can leave the building. The responsibility for closing down the hotel at night is covered, on a rota system, by key members of staff. Once they go off duty, Nick and I look after the guests during the night. Normally, we are not disturbed, but occasionally someone will telephone from America or a guest will need something, so Nick gets up. It is tiring and infuriating when we have drunken telephone calls or door bells rung by guests so intoxicated that they can't fit their keys into the hotel lock, but it has to be tolerated. We remain on duty covering the hotel until the staff return to unlock at 6.45am. If we go away, then a member of staff covers in our absence. Someone responsible is always on the premises for hotel safety and guests' requirements, day and night.

Before staff leave, they transfer the telephones through to our private house. In the bars they reconcile the evening's takings, log the till reading and remove all the money before locking the doors. Every area of the hotel has to be checked, all fire doors closed, dirty cups, glasses or trays returned to the kitchen, and the drawing room is tidied. Each lavatory, store, changing room, shower and general bathroom is inspected. The main corridor lights are left on all night, though there is emergency lighting in the event of a fire or power cut.

People become very disorientated in hotels at night. Sometimes sleepy guests may wander out of their bedrooms and then get lost or become confused. Once Nick's octogenarian great aunt Joey was staying in Room 14. During the night, another guest, a visiting priest from South Africa, accidentally wandered into her room and quietly climbed into the twin bed next to hers. Unfortunately, when he sheepishly appeared for breakfast, in full clerical dress, Joey related the night's adventure to the entire restaurant. He never returned.

The greatest danger in a hotel is fire. The bins in all the bars and restaurants must be inspected and sprinkled with water. Once each of the main areas of the ground floor are checked, the staff can finally lock the office. The latches are dropped on the front and back door, so there is no entry from outside except with a hotel key, though the door is easily opened from inside in case of an emergency. These are sacred procedures, followed in great detail.

If guests are due to arrive very late, after the hotel is locked, the front door is left open and their keys are left out in an envelope with directions to the bedroom. A list, like the passenger list on a boat, including the names everyone staying that night in the hotel, their bedroom details and whether they are out late or not yet arrived, is brought to our house, along with all the internal hotel keys. Only then can the lock up staff at last go home.

Normally this responsibility is shared between five or six key members of staff. Recently, we have been rather short and the same few have had to do extra duties. Things have become slack and the tills have not been balanced properly; there have also been some serious errors with the PDQ machine, a gadget used when customers wish to pay by credit card. We need to find a solution but initially try not to interfere. More and more Nick and I realise that if we can create an environment where the people concerned can work out their own solution, it is not only better than anything we suggest but, because it is their own idea, they find it far easier to implement. Barbara in the office quietly nannies the bar staff, in order to enable them to concentrate on what they do with their credit card slips, tills and PDQ machines and to reconcile figures before leaving at night. One possibility is for us to employ a night manager. A few years ago it would have been ridiculous for such a small hotel to run to the expense of having someone on duty in the office all night. Now we are seriously considering the possibility. Not only would it alleviate the problem with the lockup and enable us to offer a better twenty-four-hour room service, but it would also reduce the risk of fire and stop Nick having to get out of bed when he is very tired.

Ace Cleaners, a specialist company, come in to shampoo the carpets. The narrow corridor that runs the block from the front door in Seaview High Street, through the centre of the hotel, and out into the car park in Rope Walk, is a busy thoroughfare. The industrial carpet wears well, but we want to keep it up to scratch, so the cleaners come and shampoo out not only the domestic dirt, but the pints of beer, cigarette burns, food stains and wheel marks from trolleys loaded with crates that are common to any bar and restaurant. The cheerful husband-and-wife team, dressed in bright yellow overalls, work their huge machine up and down the corridor, leaving the carpet looking like new. They know the hotel well, and work their foam into the corner of each room, making everything bright and ready for the August onslaught.

The weather warms up and we prepare for the school holidays. Businessmen, with their wives and small children in tow, change into fathers in shorts. A problem from last year recurs. Children on the patio, bored while their parents dine and chat, insist on standing on the fragile wires outside the hotel. It is dangerous and it also ruins the wires, which become slack and will soon break. We try to think of what to do. The border between the hotel and the street was an old wooden fence, built by Peter Evans, the boatman at the yacht club. When we rebuilt the patio two years ago, we replaced the rotten wood with a ship's rail. The uprights were in solid shiny steel and the top, as on a yacht, was in solid hardwood. To make it look more like the side of a yacht, we also fitted stainless-steel yacht rigging wires. The wires are not a climbing frame and we know that sooner or later there is going to be a mishap. A few years ago we had a similar problem with a huge ship's anchor we found on the beach. After lugging the enormous hunk of iron up to the hotel, we painted it black and left it on the side wall of the courtyard. Children instantly started to climb up the side and we were worried that it would tip over and seriously injure one of them. So we had to transfer the anchor out of harm's way, to the back of the hotel. We can't remove the wires, so can only be vigilant and ask parents not to allow their children to climb up. The problem continues, and we keep pleading with the parents. We might have to have a solid wall or fence instead of the attractive rail and wires.

Gareth, one of the young trainee chefs, is bringing his college class to look round the hotel. We have tried to forge good working relationships with the local college and encourage young students to come and see what we do. Because of the huge skills shortage in the industry it is vital that every employer does everything possible to entice enthusiastic youngsters into the industry. We have prepared information packs and David is arranging the tour. It's important not only to us, but also to Gareth. We want him to be proud of where he is working and training and we all do our best to put on a good show.

Barbara in reception receives a call from the European Foundation for Quality Management inviting me to speak on business excellence at their conference to be held in Valencia, Spain. We are all surprised, and I am concerned that they have made some mistake. Surely they cannot really want a small hotel from the Isle of Wight to talk at a huge European conference? But they do, on 27th September. We mark it in the diary and accept, nervously. We are to fly, all expenses paid, to Barcelona and then on south to the conference venue. The Ciudad de las Artes y las Ciencias in Valencia is the Spanish equivalent of the Dome with an IMAX cinema, laserium and vast halls situated in a 900-square-metre futuristic building shaped like an eye with glass lids that can open and close. They are going to use our video from the UK winners' conference and then I am to do an eight-minute speech followed by a question-and-answer session for both of us. I try not to think about it as it seems too daunting. Still, we don't want to turn down the incredible opportunity to put not only the Seaview but also the Isle of Wight clearly on the map of Europe. We can only do our best, so we get on with the preparation for our very busy season and try not to think too much about Spain. We have the summer to get through first before being too bothered about Valencia.

We receive a call to say an inspector from the British Tourist Authority is coming to stay. Lou Casey, a representative from the BTA in Sydney, Australia, arrives to check out the hotel. She is over for a few weeks, making a tour of possible establishments that would suit Australian tourists and journalists. Nick looks after her in the restaurant during dinner and I give her all the facts and press information the following morning. She seems delighted with the hotel and is sure that our combination of a relaxed unpretentious atmosphere and high professionalism will appeal to Australians. Since we joined the Great Inns of England we have had more enquiries from all over the world but particularly from Australia. I desperately want to go out and look at their restaurants and hotels. Talking to Lou, I'm fired with enthusiasm, but wonder when we will ever have time to travel that far. Recently Charlie and I have used a number of cookbooks from Australian restaurants. They are so attractive and the food is particularly complementary to the kind of operation we run at the Seaview. I subscribe to Australian magazines like *Gourmet Traveller* and Australian *Vogue*. Their contents constantly inspire our menus while making me want to fly south. As Nick and I say goodbye to Lou, I feel I must try to make time to go before too long. Ah, well, there is always the year following the next.

★

Lynda Bellingham, the actress, is one of the main stars in the LWT series *Reach for the Moon*, currently being filmed on the Island. She and a number of the cast have become regulars at the hotel and the director has been staying with us for months. Lynda is a friend of Sally Bulloch, who worked with Nick at the Athenaeum Hotel on Piccadilly. A dedicated hotelier, she then went on to run some of the finest small hotels in central London, but recently returned to the Athenaeum. We have a great dinner party in the cottage. Sally and Nick reminisce about near disasters in the hotel when they were young. Flaming Baked Alaska being ceremoniously wheeled into private functions before the guests had finished the main course. Drunken guests, chefs and waiters. Dead bodies having to come down in the service lift to avoid the guests. The intimate details of upstairs downstairs in a London hotel. Lynda, once married to a restaurateur, really understands the business and tells some of her amusing tales and we sit up late laughing about the industry.

The back office in the reception area is too hot. The addition of various pieces of hi-tech office equipment, plus a refrigeration unit for the bar next door, have resulted in stifling conditions. It's a tiny area, but a real nerve centre, and has become a most unpleasant place to work. We have invested in several fans, but now the girls in the office are investigating the possibility of an air-conditioning unit. We know it is going to cost well over a thousand pounds, but there seems little alternative. The wall at back of the office leads on to a small passageway by Myrtle Cottage. We are going to knock through to get telephone and intercom connections between the cottage and the hotel reception and we suddenly realise that we can use an old window opening not only for the wires but also to allow fresh air into the office. It's a simple solution and we hope it will make working in the hot summer months bearable. We will see if any of the staff feel we need to take more steps. On and on, the constant need to work on the upkeep and improvement of the infrastructure.

Patrick Headlam arrives for the last of this year's Seaview wine tastings. For the first time we are holding one in the summer. Patrick works for John Armit Wines in London and has included a piece about Nick and the hotel in their new summer list; we have been buying more and more wine from them. John Armit was the wine buyer and managing director of Corney & Barrow in the seventies, and it was he who first employed me at the firm. He taught me a great deal about tasting wine and I have always admired his excellent palate. Though he was a hard taskmaster. He would sit with his feet on the desk, wearing odd stocks, fiddling with his slide rule, always looking at the margins. I was very impressionable and wanted to achieve. I would spend hours working out what I thought should be charged for wines and composing tasting notes. John always checked the margins were right. I soon learned how important profits were for a business to

Boissant 1975 which I originally bought on John Armit's recommendation with my wine allowance at C & B. The dark rich velvety pomerol is tasting very good and it is fun to share it with someone who really appreciates its depth and quality. We debate the intensity of the colour, and the maturing properties of the Merlot grape, into the small hours.

Work is continuing on the hotel's web site. We are ready to go live but are still waiting for restaurant photographer Ben Wood to take pictures of the newly decorated restaurant and other aspects of the hotel so we can use them on the site. I spend days looking through other hotel web sites, noting things I like and admire, and also the things that look awful. Slowly it is coming together. The potential is enormous and I could go on for hours each day, adding and refining what we are going to do. We have registered our name and site so now it's just a question of deciding what we want to include on each page.

While this progresses, nothing is happening with Myrtle. Now I am really getting worried. At least we know the planning has all gone through and we have possession, but no one can start work until August because they had to take on other jobs while we struggled with constant delays in the purchase. The staff go in and help themselves to anything they want in the cottage and the remainder of the furniture is donated to a refuge for the homeless in Sandown. Meanwhile I worry that at this rate we will not have the cottage ready for the autumn half term. We laughed when I took the booking for the

Millennium, thinking the cottage would be used
ages before 2000; now it is unlikely to be ready until
well into the autumn. Imagine if we had to buy a
neighbouring hotel. We don't regret Myrtle but it
has not run as smoothly as we wanted and has been
very frustrating, and has certainly lost the hotel a
considerable amount of money at the moment. We
know that in the long term it will be charming, very
popular and profitable, but that doesn't help us
now.

Mike the decorator is still painting the outside of
the hotel. We have managed to solve the problem
caused by the leaking roof in the Sunshine
Restaurant by adding white clapboard to the old
pebbledash fascia. It smartens up the side of the
hotel and also stops any water coming in. One of
the young workmen on the scaffolding, fixing the
new boards, is constantly being telephoned on his
mobile by girlfriends. In the end I have to ask him
to turn the machine off. We have already had to
apologise for any inconvenience to each of the
guests in the rooms being decorated on the outside,
but young workmen bouncing up and down on
scaffolding while discussing their social life outside
your bedroom window is just not on. Keeping the
balance between builders and guests in the winter is
not too hard, but it can be difficult when we get to
the hot summer months, with windows open and
every room occupied. Mike, our regular decorator,
is quiet and always the height of discretion, and as
he slowly carries on with his outside decorating we
manage to avoid any major upsets.

At the same time as we are decorating outside, I suddenly come up with the design for the blind we so desperately need over the glazed area of the Sunshine Restaurant. I look at so many custom-made blinds, but they are all awful. Then, while gazing up at the work outside, and checking on the young builder's arrangement of his love life, I notice the attractive blue and white wind-screens we have around three south-facing balconies. They were made by a local sail-maker, Paul Newell, and I invite him in to discuss the possibility of using the dark material, which is also used on the Seaview dinghy sails, to build a detachable blind just like one of his sails. I suggest we fit two thin metal yacht stays, so we can clip the blind on with shackles to cover the glass roof area. Paul agrees and contacts the manufacturers to get samples of sail material, in the hope that we can have the blind in place before July. The concept of a dinghy sail, in two rich and deep colours, fits perfectly into the nautical theme and design of the room. I am thrilled. In no time at all Michael Warren, the village boat builder, has fitted the wires and Paul has made the sail. Once in place it looks splendid and keeps out the bright summer sun while adding colour and depth to the room.

Pip finishes her A-level exams. Returning home pale and drained, she doesn't want to think about the results. I take her off for a night to Grayshott Hall, a health club, to calm down, relax and be spoilt like a grown-up lady of leisure. She soaks up the massages and waxes, saunas and eye-lash tints and we come back refreshed and revitalised, ready to take a short family break with Ben and Nick in the South of France. We have arranged for a few days' break, to meet up with some old friends, the Youngs, in La Napaule, to the west of Cannes. We fly to Nice and arrive at our hotel in the marina of Porte de la Rague, just round the corner from where the Youngs are staying on their yacht. We walk into the simple, modern accommodation and open the large sliding doors to step out onto our balconies with their Mediterranean views. Typically French, the doors, windows, blinds and shutters are all electronic. If I asked for simple white shutters over the windows at the Seaview, Berry Electrics would frown with disapproval and suggest it would be exorbitant. The hotel has no restaurant, so we book a table in the local brasserie next door, on the edge of the tiny port.

Nick and I survey the business at the Riviera Beach Hotel, and admire the operation. Run by a Dutch family, it is uncomplicated, inexpensive but most efficient. The hotel foyer, only yards from the beach and sea, has an attractive entrance leading to the reception area. The compact bar and large entrance lounge have tinted mirrors, cool marble floors, large comfortable sofas. There is nothing else, apart from the loos, on the ground floor. Above there are five floors of bedrooms, all with balconies and beautiful views over the sea. At roof level there is a small swimming pool built into the side of the rock, with jacuzzi and sun-deck area.

From here Nick can stand and watch the various boats, large and small, sailing off round the pretty coastline, from Monte Carlo towards Cannes and down towards St-Tropez. As they have no food operation other than providing simple continental breakfast, they are able to run on a meagre staff, and we fantasise about what it would be like to have such a simple operation in the sun. The rooms are inexpensive, less than at the Seaview. Within minutes of arriving we have established that they are fully booked and we speculate about their occupancy figures off season in this perfect location. Since the economy airline Easy Jet reduced the price of winter flights to Nice to as little as £30 we think the winter possibilities in the South of France look good.

We set off to find the restaurant where the nineteen-year-old Nick trained, the Beau Rivage, in La Napaule, but discover that it was pulled down and converted into a block of flats over twenty years ago. Nick suddenly looks deflated and feels very old. We walk on and pass the famous restaurant L'Oasis. I dined there several times with my parents during my teens and am amazed to see it has hardly changed at all. We scrutinise the menu but decide that at over £100 per person, this is one famous establishment we do not need to show our offspring.

That night, the four of us have a simple dinner in the local brasserie. Nick and I recount our experiences of living and working in restaurants and hotels on the Côte d'Azur. We dine outside lapping up delicious *moules marinière* and watching the fish wriggle in the water next to our table as we throw in bread.

The next day we take a bus into Cannes and I tell Ben and Pip about my summers with Monsieur and Madame Pujol and their eleven children at the Hôtel Spendide on the seafront. On my very first morning in Cannes, Mme Pujol took me to the fish market. We wandered up and down the aisles amongst stalls of all sorts of fish, lobsters, langoustine, prawns, mussels, oysters, huge tunas and even shark. She was making a selection of ingredients for her special fish soup. She told me how to spot if a fish was fresh by looking at its eye. Did it look at you honestly with a clear, shiny dark-black pupil, or had it grown old and milky from days away from the sea? We also went to the vegetable market to buy huge bunches of fresh herbs, strings of strong-smelling onions and giant garlic. I had never seen bunches of fresh basil and coriander with such enormous leaves, and the smell was intoxicating.

Back at the hotel Madame Pujol began to pre-pare the soup. I was staggered at the number of fat cloves of garlic she crushed to put in it – I stopped counting at twelve but it must have been nearly twenty. She ruthlessly chopped and skinned, boiled and stirred the fish and herbs. The whole operation was a precise ritual which she had performed for many years. There was no compromise, it had to be perfect. When we sat down on the balcony that first evening and I tasted the rich, pink soup with crispy toasted French bread croutons coated with the fat garlicky sauce and topped with grated cheese, my taste buds exploded. Even though I had been brought up to love and appreciate food, I discovered the French philosophy was unique. Even when up in their summer house in the mountains, the Pujols' picnics were gastronomic orgies. They would load whole trays of peaches, huge smelly ripe cheeses, crates of Rosé de Provence and baskets with home-made foie gras and crusty French bread. Then we would all march off to remote sites in stunning mountainous locations, always next to a stream. Summers with the Pujols taught me more than just French. Now back in Cannes, I am able to sit down with my own family and introduce them to the famous *soupe de poissons*.

The next day we meet the Youngs and sail out to the islands just off Cannes. Here again, I used to visit with the Pujols. Jacques, the eldest brother who was a priest, but unlike any priest I had ever met, would sail the family boat with his brothers and sisters to moor off the islands. We would then swim down and collect the black, spiky sea urchins and for lunch they would be sliced open and eaten raw with a dash of fresh lemon juice. Now, thirty years later, we enjoy a happy day swimming and sailing but avoiding the sea urchins.

After only four days we have to return to England, ready to face the six to eight weeks of the peak summer season. We gird our loins and settle back into our seats for the flight home.

While we have been away there has been a problem at the hotel. James the new barman, has walked out. Leon, the manager, has coped admirably in our absence but now we need to discover what happened, so that we can avoid this difficulty in future. It was the weekend of the Round-the-Island yacht race. This brings many visiting yachtsmen to the hotel. They are full of boisterous competition spirit and can occasionally be loud and demanding with the staff. One in particular was obnoxious last weekend and upset poor James, who rushed into the office for support from Barbara. Unfortunately, she, like everyone else, was very busy and James had to return and face the customer on his own.

The next morning he arrived for work tired and unshaven. Lee, the bar manager, not knowing of the problem the night before, asked James to shave before going into the bar. He disappeared into the staff changing rooms and emerged with cuts and blood on his collar; this had been the last straw and he walked out. 'Too many rules and regulations,' he said. We are sorry to see him go, especially as he made such a good start. He had returned to his old job at the holiday camp up the road. At least there the standards are less formal and he feels more comfortable.

Now we look at the way we recruit and train new staff. In particular, at the Friday meeting we debate at some length how much support we need to give new members of the team during their first few months. We decide that in future, in addition to their induction from David, plus their week's training in their department, they will also have a 'shadow'. That will be a long-standing member of staff who will be specifically allotted to befriend and guide the new person and to help and advise on any difficulties they may have. It is not only worrying to lose James at this stage of the summer, but also very expensive. We want to learn from this problem.

Charlie, Bob and I debate the new summer menu. This is the most difficult selection of the year: it has to be workable in peak season. The wrong dish can cause havoc on a busy night. For this menu, we don't have a brainstorming session with all the younger chefs, as none of them has actually experienced the pressure of August at the Seaview. Charlie, Bob, Tom and I know it all too well. Over the past few weeks they have been trying out a number of potential recipes as specials on Saturday nights. The aim is to assess how popular the dish is with guests, how difficult it is to prepare and cook on a busy evening and how it fits in with the other dishes in order to give a complete and well-balanced selection.

Breast of chicken, always popular, is stuffed with a goats' cheese mousse, steamed and then served on a bed of hot shredded beetroot and sour cream. The combination of flavours is delicious, it is relatively quick and easy to prepare and a certain addition to the new menu. For August, we always serve Bembridge lobster, whether cold with salad and mayonnaise or hot with lemon butter or traditional thermidor. Sea bass and fresh local crab-meat, either made into crab cakes or lightly dressed cold with salad are added as specials when available. With the warm summer days, dining al fresco is a regular event, be it for breakfast, lunch or dinner, and we increase the number of cold salad starters. Lou Bland at Marks & Spencer told us in April to add traditional Caesar salad with fresh anchovies to the menu and now it a huge success. It was also Lou's suggestion that we subscribe to the Australian food magazines, and this has been an inspiration to Charlie, and the chefs.

We have fun preparing the menus, knowing that the restaurant will be virtually full every night and the clientele are both discerning and adventurous diners. They crave variety and versatility. Charlie's delicious smoked haddock and prawn chowder was slow to move on the spring menu, but is now very popular. With so many new restaurants around us, we have much more competition; so it's even more important to get the balance of the menu right. We juggle with dishes and flavours, ingredients and preparation times and come out with the final product. The menu looks good and is printed ready for 1st July.

CHAPTER 10

July
Hot and Hassled

A small hotel, the Birdham in Bembridge, is for sale. Three years ago we made an offer on the property and now the agent rings to see if we are still interested. This throws us into a quandary. We have been investing in tiny Myrtle Cottage – but another whole hotel? The business has a lucrative but different bar trade, fourteen bedrooms, twelve with private bath and a large garden and car park. The town of Bembridge is bigger than Seaview with a sheltered harbour, two sailing clubs, good shops, six public houses, a large residential population and similar summer clientele.

The purchase price is remarkably cheap but the business has serious problems. The hotel hasn't a particularly good reputation and a group of heavy drinkers dominate the public bar. While this is good for the tills it would be hard to supervise from five miles away. Nick and I are preparing for the very busy month of August, but find ourselves constantly distracted by the possibility of running the Birdham. Everything says we should go for it.

When we looked at the property three years ago we drew up a business plan and estimated the cost of refurbishment. Nick digs out the old file, remembering that the building and electrics are structurally good. The main expense will be the kitchen. Hardly anything in a commercial kitchen costs less than a thousand pounds, not even the toaster. Every table, shelf and drawer needs to be in stainless steel, which these days is like solid silver. Each commercial oven and refrigeration unit costs as much as a family car and by the time you have bought the whole range or built a walk-in fridge, you are into a Rolls-Royce. Then there are the essential ventilation systems, smoke extraction, fire precautions and special non-slip, heavy-duty floor.

A commercial kitchen is a production line, continuously creating a high-quality product. It needs considerable initial investment in the latest technology and equipment to save on labour and get food out fast. You need at least £50,000 for just the basic set-up. Then you need all the extras – knives and sharpening steels, giant pots and copper pans, mincers and juicers and mixers, at least another £10,000.

Previously we had planned to close the Birdham, both to carry out the refurbishment and to change its image, and then to re-open as the Bembridge Hotel, twinned with the Seaview. On rethinking the plan, it looks plausible and workable. Situated centrally, but some way from the sea, we still believe the whole property is well worth the market price of £225,000. Interestingly, a private house in the area with far less garden would cost more. We are definitely tempted.

What holds us back is the question, Do we need

the hassle? When we bought the Seaview we were in our twenties. Now in our late forties, with a thriving business and feeling very contented, if harried, we have to think carefully before taking a step like this. Why take on another business twenty minutes' drive away that can only cause increased stress and problems? We ponder the opportunity.

The agent asks us to keep our 'first refusal' confidential until August, but after that we will need to move quickly. We arrange a meeting with Andrew Porteus, our accountant, and talk to our friendly bank manager, Steve Cook. Finances are not a problem. We can raise the money if we need it. Our fear is that the first week in August is Cowes Week, one of the busiest weeks of the year and not really a time for us to be rushing into big decisions on a new venture. Normally I can make a business decision very quickly but this one has me in a real quandary. Perhaps I should consult our horoscope for an answer.

We run over the pros and cons. If we take on the Birdham it would enable us to promote and give added responsibility to the young team constantly developing at the Seaview. Because we are so small, we can't promote the management within the business, so junior staff regrettably have to move on if they want to move up. We have expanded and developed the Seaview to capacity, while the Bembridge Hotel would offer an interesting challenge with plenty of scope. For success, we know the Seaview formula and need only apply it elsewhere. The Birdham claims a turnover of £300,000 and we believe we could improve on that in a relatively short time. A quick guide to valuing a hotel is one and a half times turnover, so the Birdham looks cheap. Finally, both the large car park and the garden behind offer potential for development.

The main problem is that bar, with its reputation. We could shut the public bar and turn it into a quiet residents' lounge in order to avoid any problems. That would not be easy and might cause resentment in the town. Then there are staff shortages. We struggle to get enough good employees now, so we would be doubling our difficulties. Two separate businesses would spread our resources and could dilute the quality of what we offer at Seaview. More than anything, Nick and I wonder why we would want to take on such a big challenge at this stage in our life. The thinking continues through July and we poll the staff and our family.

Jim Tory joins us as bar manager. The Tory family are close friends and Jim and Ben were best mates at boarding school. Recently Jim was working as a trainee bar manager in a hotel in Dorset. Nick received several anxious telephone calls from his father Steve, concerned about how disillusioned his son had become as a result of the poor pay, long hours and difficult working conditions Jim was forced to endure. Hotels need to be manned twenty-four hours a day, seven days a week. It is hard for the operators to keep the staff workload within respectable hours. All too often enthusiastic trainees, like junior doctors, are forced to work over sixty hours a week. When we first married, Nick was sometimes on duty for a full five days, Monday to Friday, including additional evening shifts, and then had to be the resident manager day and night for the whole weekend. On the Monday morning he had to continue to work the following week with no time off in lieu. It was hard, and though as the owners we still endure excessive hours ourselves, we have eliminated this exhausting practice for our employees at the Seaview.

Steve was worried about his son, who was not only asked to work excessive hours but also expected to take on considerable responsibility without adequate training. This is almost a text-book profile of a huge blot in our industry: Jim found the pressure too much. Disillusioned, he decided to leave after only a short time, and we offered him a job. There is a position running the front bar and sharing management responsibility with Lee. We can give Jim a good solid training, attractive pay and conditions, plus the promise of a basic forty-hour week, with a maximum of forty-eight. Jim has jumped at the chance and we are all relieved and delighted to have him join us.

The advantage for the hotel is that we know Jim. He helped his mother in her catering business for years and is honest, hard-working and keen. More important, after the problems with James in the front bar, and with the summer rush under way, we know Jim will not get flustered and will be able to charm even the most demanding of yachties. His only problem may be trying to supervise our daughter Pip, as she is working in the front bar too.

The summer students arrive for the four to six weeks of the peak season. At the bus station in Ryde, Jim and Ben meet Gaëlle, a pretty French girl, struggling with her luggage while searching for the bus to Seaview. The young men fall over each other to offer assistance, and are delighted when they discover this attractive student will be spending the summer working at the hotel to improve her English. Ben gets a chance to use his French chat-up lines learned in Bordeaux, while Jim looks forward to helping her come to grips with serving in his bar. Gaëlle, meanwhile, smiles as enchantingly as she will all summer.

As each new member of staff arrives, we are pleased to see that the new shadow system is working well. One young trainee, on a New Deal government training scheme, has a medical problem. Sarah, her shadow, is able to support her through the worrying time, and also liaise with us. Puji, a foreign student from Sri Lanka, here on a two-year work placement studying hotel management at our local college, is concerned about training in the restaurant. We appoint Puji himself to supervise the new members of the team after their initial induction. It's good management experience for him and should result in a more efficient and professional service for all.

Josh flies in from the Blue Mountain Hotel School in Sydney. He is here to start a six-month work placement. This highly professional school contacted us several months ago as a result of publicity about our unusual management practices. It is beneficial to the business to have enthusiastic young trainees, and we learn from them as they do from us. Over recent months Josh and I have been communicating by email and it is good to meet him in person. He quickly settles in, along with all the other new recruits. We are particularly lucky this season, as all the students make an excellent start and are highlighted in the minutes of the weekly meeting. One advantage for us in employing a student like Josh is that he brings new exciting ideas to the business. So often student placements are used to cover menial tasks and just as plate carriers. What we have discovered is that these young people are full of the latest ideas in the industry and can teach us so much. We try to give both Josh and Puji the opportunity to experiment with their ideas at the Seaview, so we can all benefit.

With the influx of staff comes an increase in the number of staff meals. Each evening before producing the restaurant and bar food, Charlie and the chefs cook dinner for all the resident employees. Between six and six thirty they all sit down together in the Sunshine Restaurant. It's not easy for the chefs to produce a different evening meal each night and still try to please everyone's different tastes, particularly when they are under pressure to prepare for the restaurant food. They do their best, but Leon is concerned that there are not enough fresh vegetables and, like modern school dinners, too many of the ever popular chips. We decide to offer fresh fruit with each meal, to give vitamins and balance.

Another problem aggravated in the summer is smoking. During their breaks in the heat of the day, the staff want to get out of the building. At the back of the hotel we have three bedrooms, and it is just not acceptable to have young chefs puffing away outside guests' rooms. We ask the smokers to keep out of sight and away from the bedrooms, but, more important, we try to insist they sweep up their dog-ends. They don't always. We badly need a staff room.

Dan, the new breakfast chef, becomes a father. His wife gives birth to baby Isla and now Dan needs time off to be with them. Since he recently joined us, he has needed odd days to support his wife, but now needs paternity time to get the family settled. We all understand and are delighted for Dan, but the hotel guests also need their cooked breakfasts. The others chefs rally round and work extra hours to cover for his absence. It is hard on them when the hotel is already so busy.

New employment legislation, designed to support employees' rights, enables them to have family time or go sick and not worry about their position. Nick and I have always tried to be sympathetic to all our employees' needs, and we believe in the need to protect workers' rights, especially from unscrupulous employers, even though for a small business it is hard to cover when a member of the team is away. The chefs brave the added burden of covering Dan's shifts and celebrate the birth of Isla, while we send off a bouquet to Dan's wife and new baby.

As the sun shines and the temperature rises, vital equipment starts to go on the blink. It happens every year. Today we have problems with the hot-water still, which makes all the hotel coffee and tea. Early in the morning the restaurant is full of guests waiting for their breakfast, while others are still up in their bedrooms expecting their early-morning tea or coffee to be delivered along with their news-paper. Puji digs out the old coffee machine from the store, while kettles are quickly filled. When we refurbished the kitchen we replaced an old hot-water urn that had cost £150 with a new, state-of-the-art, £2,500 multi-functional piece of equip-ment. From the start it never worked properly and Nick constantly complains to both the supplier and manufacturer. We have already spent a fortune calling out the engineer and installing new parts. Now, at one of the busiest times of year, the machine fails us again. It is as temperamental and infuriating as an old geyser.

Next, one of the beer coolers breaks down, followed by the air-conditioning unit in the back restaurant, which is not cooling the room suffi-ciently. The machine to squeeze the orange juice for breakfast stops and now the large industrial washing machine is up the spout. We have to make quick decisions. A new washing machine and another air-conditioning unit will cost over £2,000 each, but are ordered, while the other machines are repaired. Meanwhile, all the usual services we offer our guests must continue uninterrupted. No one must know there are these troubles in the works.

In fairness, the old washing machine has done us proud. Initially, like most hotels, we sent our dirty linen to a laundry. Then, following an incident at the laundry in which our entire stock of brand-new tablecloths was ruined by over-bleaching, we decided to do the work in-house and installed our own equipment. That was over ten years ago and since then the big old machine has washed thousands of sheets, pillowcases, tablecloths and napkins. We converted an old ground-floor loo to build the small hotel laundry. Every day that the hotel is full, the machines wash over thirty-two sheets, sixty-four pillowcases, thirty-two bath and hand towels, not to mention individual bathrobes. From morn to night the equipment is in use. In addition, it also has to cope with more than thirty white linen tableclothes, eighty-odd napkins, all the checked breakfast cloths and hundreds of dirty tea towels left over from the wash-up and bar glasses the night before. Each item has to be sorted, put through the washing machine on the correct cycle, transferred to the huge gas tumble drier and then carefully pressed in the industrial roller iron.

The laundry is manned seven days a week, in cramped, hot conditions. The responsibility is shared predominantly by Mary and Wendy, with extra help at the weekend. Unfortunately, Wendy had an operation in the spring and has now been off sick for months. Fay, the head housekeeper, has been juggling to try to cover the extra duties, but now, with the hotel full to capacity every night, the strain on the laundry and housekeeping is beginning to tell. The last thing they need is the main washing machine out of action, so we take the plunge and order a new one.

A guest's name is rubbed out of the reservations book. His room is then relet to another gentleman. Nobody knows who made the mistake but Mr Smith is due to arrive and we don't have a room for him. Nick goes pale. He personally deals with Mr Smith, who undoubtedly is not happy. We have reserved a similar room in a pleasant hotel less than three miles away and Nick offers to pay for a taxi, but that will not do as the guest is sailing in Seaview and wants to be in the village. So we find him a room at the Northbank Hotel across the road. It doesn't have a private bath, but at least it is in Seaview and Nick apologises profusely while he escorts Mr Smith across the road and carries his bags. That evening the guest returns for dinner in the restaurant and seems happy with the new arrangements. Nick heaves a huge sigh of relief.

This is not the kind of error we can afford to repeat. Barbara takes careful note to speak to all the staff on the reception and to ensure nothing like this ever happens again. The reservations book is constantly changing. In the margin are the rooms and along the top of each page is the date. Names are added and removed as guests telephone to make first provisional and then confirmed reservations. On any day each page will change countless times, so every entry is written in pencil. Small letters appear by each booking: TBC meaning 'to be confirmed', Def. for a definite booking, a letter Z for an extra bed for a child or D B & B meaning dinner, bed and breakfast as opposed to B & B. Regular guests book the same room from year to year, others have never been to the hotel before and don't know what to expect. Some like to move around and we have regulars who have tried nearly every room in the place. Whatever the booking, we try to get the details right and feel bad about the mistake with Mr Smith.

July is a mixture of rain, wind and a heatwave. On one of our days off, Nick and I are invited to a very genteel lunch party and croquet match with some old friends who live in the Old Rectory on the west of the Island in Shorwell. We were sent a formal invitation weeks ago with full details including the rules of the game and exactly what to wear. It makes a refreshing break from the busy hotel. We arrive at the beautiful old stone house and are escorted into the Cecils' garden for an al fresco lunch before the match. The garden, situated on the side of a hill, is split into a series of levels, the top with a swimming pool, the second with a terrace and greenhouse and the remainder each with its own tidy lawn and surrounding roses and shrubs. The sun is baking and we are grateful for the elderflower cordial and chilled white wine.

We lunch on cold salmon, lightly minted new potatoes, and Island strawberries and cream. Then our host, Os Cecil, uses his old Panama hat to draw for the teams, and after coffee we are each sent off to one of the carefully laid out croquet pitches. The heat is almost unbearable on a sweltering afternoon, yet this very English gathering determinedly knock their balls through hoops while sending their opponents' balls off course into rose bushes or down steep banks. I am no great player and our hostess Lady Cecil and her partner win the first round. Meanwhile Nick, on another lawn, is doing better, in spite of being initially slightly taken aback when he politely avoided sending our host's ball packing only to have his own booted well off pitch. We play three rounds and there is much confusion about the final score, so we all retire exhausted for lemonade and delicious home-made coffee sponge cake.

My croquet partner is Christopher Bland, an old family friend and the Island's Lord Lieutenant. He and Nick share a love of machines and old engines. Chris owns and flies his own Tiger Moth aeroplane and offers to take me up for a spin. So a few days later, on another sunny day, I find myself goggled up and peeking over the side of the flying machine, looking down on Seaview. We have flown over Bembridge and the Birdham Hotel, the harbour and round the bay to the Priory Hotel and then Seaview. It certainly helps to put our business and future plans in perspective, looking at things at a different angle from this overview above.

We noisily turn this way and that, my tummy tingles and I struggle to get my bearings and recognise the locations as we move across the whole

Island. The heavily built-up and populated sections seem relatively small and it is so obvious from the air why half the Island is designated an Area of Outstanding Natural Beauty. I clearly pick out the downlands where we ride with the horses and each cove and inlet I know so well.

July is the month for outdoor extravaganzas and open-air concerts. We fly over the grounds of Queen Victoria's home, Osborne House, and can see the preparation for the open-air classical concert and firework display that evening. The grand old house and gardens, formally laid out, look most impressive when seen from above. We fly on to Chris's house at Yafford, near the sea on the west side of the Island, and gently land in a field to be met by Nick, Jules and Chris's wife Judith Bland. This has been a thrilling way to get the lay of the land, and fires me with enthusiasm as we drive back to Seaview discussing the possibilities for expanding the business.

I visit Dimbola House in Freshwater to see a summer exhibition of David Bailey's photographs. Margaret Cameron, the early Victorian photographer, owned the house, close to Tennyson's home at Farringford. The building, now a photographic museum, has spectacular views down to the sea and up over Tennyson Down. A number of our guests, particularly Americans, ask for information about Dimbola, so I want to see their latest exhibition in order to be able to give the right facts and information. I try to regularly visit all the

Island's main attractions to keep up to date.

I walk into the empty room and stand back and admire David Bailey's black-and-white portraits of sixties icons. A darker side of Island history is reflected in a picture of the Kray brothers. They spent time in Parkhurst prison and Violet, their mother, along with other family members and friends, became regular Island visitors. I leave the pictures of Mick Jagger and Jack Nicholson and wander into a room containing copies of the elaborate Victorian compositions of Margaret Cameron herself and contrast them with the simplicity of Bailey's work. There is a strong feeling of peace and history in the house and I'm pleased I made the effort to drive across the Island. After lunch in the vegetarian restaurant, whose menu is influenced by the late Linda McCartney – she was, through Kodak, a sponsor of the museum – I drive back along the coastal road in brilliant sunshine.

We are having a problem with the printed menus. The restaurant is busy and diners in both restaurants all want to sit down at the same time. This means that in spite of having over fifty large navy-blue folders containing the full restaurant menu, we sometimes run out of spares. It is frustrating for the staff, as guests arrive and there are no free copies available to offer. Others, who have nearly finished their meal, nonchalantly chat while choosing their pudding. We can't force them to hurry up and order. We either need to have more new menu covers for this peak period or to come up with another solution.

Following inspiration from our friends at Launceston Place, I decide to print a separate menu with just the puddings, savouries, cheese, sweet dessert wines and port. I sort out the layout on the computer, select a colour photograph of a yacht, and rush over to the printers in Newport. Percy, at Pronta-Print, once again speedily rushes through the job and gets each new menu heat-sealed and delivered back to the hotel for dinner that night. The problem is solved and all our diners can chat away for as long as they like before ordering. I have learned over the years that it is vital to have a good working relationship with our printers, just like all our other suppliers. Percy is used to me rushing in and needing something yesterday. He understands how we work at the Seaview and always manages to come up trumps.

I am invited to the launch of the new English Tourism Council at the Mandarin Hyde Park Hotel with Chris Smith the Culture Secretary and Janet Anderson, Minister for tourism and film. The last thing I want to do on a hot sunny day in July is to go up to London. But having watched the government implement the regional changes and transformation of the old English Tourist Board, I feel I ought to be there.

Walking up from the underground I spot the familiar face of Patricia Yates, from *Holiday Which?*, and we team up to face the crowd. As we mount the grand entrance to the hotel we are greeted by smiling girls with the statutory Welcome pack, before being directed into a crowded room where the schedule suggests we 'network'. That word again! In the midst of our busy summer season, I had forgotten how much I hate these silly words. Patricia congratulates me on being so confident and going up and chatting to everyone. I'm staggered, as I always think I'm hopeless outside my own establishment, but we both network on.

Before the big rush we venture into the main auditorium and sit at the front to get a good view. Chris Smith starts the speeches, then he and Janet Anderson promptly leave. I am amazed. I thought they would at least stay for part of the morning but they're off in a matter of minutes. The other speeches go on and on and by the third I am day-dreaming about Bembridge and not able to listen to any more of the vast array of statistics. Chris Smith definitely had the right idea. Finally, the presentation is over and we are allowed out for lunch. I talk to Ken Robinson about the possibility of the Island hovercraft being used to transport people to the Millennium Dome. Ken is very much the man behind the Dome and he explains all the problems. I know that Chris Bland, who is one of the directors of Hovertravel and Hoverwork, will be interested, as he has been trying to investigate the possibilities of hovering visitors down the Thames to the Dome. Ken explains the numbers involved and I get lost in the figures again. That evening I go to see Cate Blanchett in David Hare's play *Plenty*, followed by dinner at the famous Ivy Restaurant. Both are cultural and catering revelations compared to the rather turgid atmosphere of the morning conference.

The summer sailing courses held at the Sea View Yacht Club start in July, with Adult Sailing Week. Ben is ensconced down at the club in his new position of senior instructor. At lunchtime and in the evening the hotel restaurants are full of tired sailing novices chatting about points of sail and wind on tide, while young instructors mix with the locals in the public bar. The sea below the hotel is now specked with an array not only of the Seaview dinghies but also with huge rubber RIBs with powerful engines, local fishing boats and countless other vessels large and small. From the top of the high street locals and visitors alike gaze out at the numerous activities on the water.

The local fishermen are out day and night trying to meet the demand for crab, lobster, prawns and sea bass. Charlie has to be careful to ensure that we have a constant supply, along with plaice and lemon sole. It can be difficult, because before the fishermen can bring their catch up to the hotel, other visitors meet them at the water's edge to offer London prices for their delicacies. Charlie has to remind the fishermen that the hotel is always loyal and constantly uses them, so they ensure we are not left short.

Other hotel suppliers are under pressure. Deliveries coming from the mainland are held up with the sheer volume on the ferries. Local suppliers get stuck in traffic and can't get to the hotel at their usual time. They arrive late in the afternoon when all the staff are off duty and the receptionists are not able to accept buckets of live lobster or twenty crates of wine. It's a problem but we compromise, knowing that in a few weeks all will return to normal.

The cadet sailing course begins. Cars, unable to park in the crowded streets, are now held up by parents and young sailors pushing dinghies on heavy trailers down the roads to the sea. Noisy adolescents, busy on the water all day, then search for entertainment at night. This is the beginning of a difficult time for the hotel. We must not serve alcohol to anyone under eighteen or allow them to consume it on the hotel premises. The yacht club cadets are not eighteen. They come to the hotel in large groups and sit in the courtyard. They then send in an older youth to buy a large round and hope that we won't notice who is drinking what. If the barman refuses to give the youth drinks for the youngsters outside, they then bring in their own bottles of alcohol and merely ask for water at the bar. Either way, Nick's licence and the hotel's future is at risk. When we built the new restaurant partially in the courtyard, we reduced the size of the problem. It also meant that parents sitting in our restaurant were able to see exactly what their young were up to outside. Luckily this year we are no longer the favourite venue of the under-age drinkers and we remain relatively free of late-night drinking cadets. From Cadet Week onwards, the club lays on a series of parties and dances and social activities for its younger members. But having had three teenagers myself, I know that the real excitement takes place on the beach.

The month finishes with another great article in the *Sunday Times*. On the front of the Travel section is a huge, two-page piece in colour, entitled 'Wight Magic'. Not only does it credit us as the best hotel on the Island but there is a long piece about the beauty of Ventnor, which includes an excellent write-up on my brother William's hotel, the Royal. The phones ring constantly with enquiries and all the guests staying this weekend are thrilled. William and I find that more and more we are sharing customers, who like to spend time in the two very different resorts and contrasting family hotels. We are delighted with the article and add it to the press file.

The bookings for July have been high, as usual. The occupancy in the bedrooms is up, as is the turnover, by nearly 8.8 per cent, well above inflation. But with the heavy capital investment in new plant and machinery we will need a steady growth. One worry is that the restaurant covers are slightly down. It is a small decline, but one we don't ignore. We suspect that with so many new restaurants opening in the area, people are exercising their greater choice. We know that while the rise in the standard of food and accommodation available on the Island is good for everyone, the initial effect of the influx of new establishments will inevitably be to take trade from us. Having taken the business from a low turnover to an exceptionally high figure, we now have to decide what to do next. It just is not possible to fit more people into the sixteen bedrooms or take more money in the crowded bars. In fact, during this busy month we constantly need to assure that as the pressure increases, the standards do not fall. So taking on Bembridge becomes an increasingly attractive proposition.

John Burleigh, our independent business consultant, sends his annual report on the hotel. It is very positive and constructive but points out one or two areas for concern. He wants us to think about our long-term plans for the future. He points out that while room occupancy is still increasing it is less marked than in previous years. The bars and restaurant show a slight increase but certainly at busy periods we seem to have reached our capacity. He also tells us that many businesses that have won quality awards then slide into the red, having reached their peak. We don't want that to happen. Nick and I carefully study the details and again think of the important decision we now have to make regarding the purchase of the hotel in Bembridge. We have to face it and make up our minds.

CHAPTER 11

August
High Days and Holidays

The beginning of August is Cowes Week, one of the oldest and most famous sailing regattas in the world. The Island is invaded by the great and the good, the richest and the fastest afloat. Everyone wants to see and be seen on the Solent. Below the hotel the water is crowded with hundreds of boats of every shape and size. You can tell the serious yachtsmen by their gnarled hands and bronzed wrinkled complexions. They appear in faded docksider shoes, shorts belted round the waist with worn rope attached to a trusty sailor's knife and marlin spike and above baggy rugby-style tops with old caps and sunglasses twinkling white with salt spray. The fashionable set shed their Ascot finery and Henley blazers for reefer jackets and yachting caps.

The hotel is full. Regular guests who have become old friends arrive and Nick and I welcome them back like hosts at a large house party. Every berth and bed in Cowes is booked and the town is teeming day and night. Others choose to avoid the throng and stay in quieter retreats elsewhere on the Island. Early each morning the tables outside the hotel are occupied by competitors discussing the day's tactics while stoking up on a hotel breakfast before setting off for Cowes. The drive from Seaview, normally twenty minutes, now takes nearly an hour. By speedboat it's less, and the stretch of water leading into Cowes marina is bubbling with the spray from hundreds of commuting mariners motoring in from up and down the coast.

It is the best and worst time of year for us. The hotel is frantically busy every night, but with all the new summer staff Nick and I can afford to take time off during the day. We are invited to join a lunch party at the Royal Yacht Squadron, so, after ensuring all the hotel guests are happy at breakfast, we too set off for Cowes, arriving before the yacht racing starts. We wander through the narrow crowded streets brightly coloured with flags and bunting, down to the promenade and a string of famous old yacht clubs, the Royal London, Royal Corinthian and, right on the seafront, the Royal Yacht Squadron. Along the pavement by each pontoon huge billboards boast special pleasure-boat rides out to see the magnificent visiting yachts and the start of the day's racing. We look out to sea and notice the sorrowful gap where *Britannia* and her naval escort used to lie. In the past queues would form, but today there is little demand without the attraction of the majestic old yacht. Prince Philip is still in Cowes along with other celebrities including Jane Fonda who is reputedly staying on a large square rigger.

We arrive at the Squadron gates and collect our

badges allowing us access to the lawn and marquee where we are to lunch. We leave the crowds and walk up under the canopy on to the grass immediately in front of the start-line. There we meet the Aishers, old friends and loyal customers, and discuss the conditions for today's racing. As the starting guns fire each class of yachts streams over the line and off into the Solent, first the Maxis, then the Swans, followed by the Hunters and Bembridge Redwings. As the Sea View Mermaids line up for their start we spot many familiar faces aboard, anxiously attempting to get the best position.

Here on dry land we turn to see a number of our Cowes Week regulars arrive to join their own lunch parties. In particular Paul Methuen, one of our senior and more colourful regular hotel guests. Paul, immaculately dressed and behaving impeccably as always, like the Squadron is part of another era.

Each year just before the start of Cowes, Paul arrives to stay with us at the hotel for nearly a month. Fay has carefully stored away all his yachting clothes which are now brought out ready to be placed in his room on arrival. Paul has been a serious competitor both at Cowes and Seaview since his childhood in the 1920s. Now a spectator from the Squadron lawn, he returns each day after racing finishes in Cowes, to compete in the Seaview evening dinghy race.

Nick, spotting many hotel customers, has to restrain himself from greeting them as though he was back at Seaview. In the marquee we meet

Paul's brother, another great character, who, while we watch a team of Australian yachtsmen, nonchalantly recounts the tale of a disreputable British aristocrat, with a criminal record as a result of his drug habit, being denied entry into Australia. The haughty young man told the Australian immigration official he thought being a convict was obligatory for entry to that particular continent.

In brilliant sunshine and with a good breeze we watch the exciting competition at sea while enjoying iced coffee and Pimms, followed by a buffet lunch. Our party, hosted by John and Susanna Chandler, is made up of friends from Seaview and Bembridge. It is a refreshing pleasure for us to be served in such dignified and civilised surroundings. As the afternoon progresses the final guns fire as different yacht classes race to the finishing line immediately in front of the Squadron.

There have been complaints this year about the bang of the race guns. Some wish the local authority to ban their use, as they find them too loud and a noise infringement. Paul Methuen and the Squadron members cannot begin to understand what all the fuss is about – times are definitely changing. In the marquee a string quartet strikes up and tea is served from a huge silver urn. We leave the 'ancient regime' of the Royal Yacht Squadron and wander back through the jostling crowds to return for a night's hard work at the Seaview.

Each evening, not only Paul Methuen, but other Seaview yachtsmen rush back from Cowes in time to compete in the evening dinghy race. The sea wall by the yacht club is lined with families and friends watching their sons, daughters, brothers, sisters, husbands and fathers, row out to one of the 180 dinghies moored off the yacht club slip. The boats are all individually built by the Warren family. The wiry figure of Michael Warren, with his wild black hair, is seen pacing up and down the esplanade trying to fix every problem shackle or broken tiller before the race – it's an impossible task. Meanwhile his young son Nick is afloat rowing out to fix another mooring. Michael's father, known as Bunny, spent his life employing and passing on the traditional boat-building skills used to craft the twelve-foot clinker dinghies from oak, mahogany and Canadian spruce. Just before Bunny died he stood on the sea wall with his son and grandson and watched a special fiftieth anniversary race of the one-design class. In one incredibly touching moment the three generations saw their entire life's work float before their eyes.

Wobbling about on the moorings the helms unveil the brightly coloured sails and set the jibs free. Then just after six o'clock the final gun goes and they are off, heading for the first mark. The competition of international yachtsmen in Cowes has nothing on the fierce rivalry that takes place on the waters off Seaview. Brother fights brother for first place around the buoy – cries of 'Starboard!' and 'Water!' echo over the waves, along with other unrepeatable expletives ignored by seagulls, as the cumbersome little boats bob round the rusty coloured buoys out at sea. By seven thirty tonight's winner is celebrating.

The totally unique Seaview dinghies have much in common with the Seaview hotel. Very small, resulting in cramped and bruised legs and sore wet bottoms, they are not easy to sail. They are dwarfed next to the giant corporate maxi racing yachts at Cowes, just as we were overshadowed by the huge corporations in last winter's UK Quality Awards. The boats have a particular appeal and charm all of their own and are treasured by each helm. Yet as we struggle to hold our particular appeal against the meteoric rise of the budget travel inns that have blossomed all over the country, so the old Seaview one design now has to compete with the flash, mass-produced, zippy fibreglass racing dinghies that thrill the young today. I wonder sometimes how long the old-fashioned skills of the Warrens and the individual service of the Haywards will survive in the twenty-first century.

Tired and wet competitors climb back up the hill to change while I greet the smartly dressed early diners and show them to their tables. Taking the orders, I soon realise which are the most popular dishes on the menu. This season's hit, especially with the returning sailors, is bubble and squeak, topped with poached egg, crispy bacon and mustard sauce.

We have no dress code at the Seaview, but there can be a distinct contrast in different guests' attire, especially during August. Some arrive in mess kit, dinner jackets or white tie and tails, off after dinner to smart parties or yacht club summer balls, while others, after rowing ashore having sailed from the mainland and moored off Seaview, appear in their rather damp shorts. We treat everyone the same, though I love to see the parade of glamorous gowns at this time of year.

Where you sit in the restaurant becomes all-important. The window table in the front, or the round table, clearly visible under the model of the French naval destroyer in the Sunshine Restaurant, are both favourites. Some diners wait until everyone else arrives to ensure maximum impact when parading through the restaurant, others like to sit quietly tucked away in a corner and observe. Large parties often change their numbers, so we add and subtract places, only to find that having brought in and laid up a special table with extra settings, half the party decides not to come. We smile through gritted teeth and say 'No trouble at all.' Then another group increase their numbers and want to squeeze eight round a table that will realistically only take the original six that booked. Nick, in his never-ending desire to please everyone, simply adds more chairs so the confused staff do their best, though they find it impossible to keep up our normal standards when the table is so crowded.

The noise level in the restaurants rises as the month progresses, particularly under the low ceiling in the Sunshine, and becomes almost unbearable. We find it hard to hear the orders, as do many of the diners, so we usher the quieter guests up to the calm of the drawing room for coffee, to avoid the raucous nature of the larger parties.

247

Sunday evening during Cowes Week, we arrive on duty at seven o'clock when the bars open, to find every table on the terrace outside already taken. It has been a sweltering day and the water in Priory Bay was heaving with hundreds of boats loaded to the gunwales with family parties. The sandy beach has been crowded and ringing with voices shouting instructions for the games of cricket or rounders, while the smell of sizzling barbecues filled the air. The well-kept secret of this enchanting place has clearly gone forever and up through the trees the new Oyster Restaurant at the Priory Bay Hotel is packed.

Now, as the sun goes down, we know we are going to be busy too. Every member of staff is charged and ready to go pulling pints and wine corks, taking down complicated orders with numerous specials on the side, rushing to get extra chairs and tables from the store, the lounge and finally our house next door. The hotel is busting at the seams, vibrant and alive. Every member of the team seems to excel in whatever they do. One particularly demanding lady in the front bar informs Pip that she is a personal friend of Nick Hayward and needs special treatment immediately. Pip politely informs the customer that unfortunately she will have to wait her turn.

The food looks good and with such a large, discerning clientele the investment in expensive local seafood delicacies is paying off. Not only outside, but inside too, the bars are packed with diners squashed round the tiny tables, dining on lobster and chips washed down with bottles of Cloudy Bay or champagne. There is a delay at the peak time around nine. The order board in the kitchen is full to capacity, with each docket representing a table of diners waiting in anticipation for their food. The chefs sizzle with the steaks as they furiously get through each order. The waiting staff manage to carry the heavy trays laden with the complicated orders outside and desperately search for the correct party. Everyone eventually is satiated with food while Nick bobs from table to table checking nothing has been left off their order and that everyone is happy. The crowds of diners eat up the vibrant party atmosphere.

The bar shutters come down at ten thirty, but in spite of Sunday licensing hours, we are still encouraging the last to leave at nearly midnight. Then we start sweeping up the mess and dog-ends before laying up the tables for breakfast and ensuring the ground floor is clean and tidy ready for the early risers. Most nights, when everything is finished, Nick and I walk down to Quay Rocks and sit on the sea wall, quietly calming down after the hectic evening and watching the gentle rock of the water below before turning back up the hill to retire to bed. Tonight we sit amazed – the sea is covered with hundreds of red, green and white lights. Each one represents a boat that has sailed round and moored off Seaview and Priory Bay for the night. We will be busy tomorrow.

While the Admiral's Cup yachtsmen compete round the marks in Cowes, Opi sailing week takes place in Seaview. During the day the village is overrun with small children and their white fibre-glass, bathtub sailing boats, called Optimists. Smartly kitted up eight- and nine-year-olds, march down in their junior docksiders to the yacht club slip. Ben and a group of other instructors help launch the line of intrepid sailors, half drowned by their cumbersome life jackets. The tiny vessels bob off from the slip one at a time, watched by what the young instructors refer to as 'yummy mummies'.

During their midday break the families hurry up to the hotel for the young yachtsmen to lunch on scampi and chips with lashings of tomato ketchup, while the mummies dine on Caesar salad with anchovies. The kitchen has to quickly produce each order so that the Optimist sailors can be back afloat for the afternoon's instruction. Then at teatime, tired and wet, still smothered in their life jackets, they return for boiled eggs and Marmite soldiers, before going to bed exhausted.

This year Cowes Week is followed by the solar eclipse. Our friends Howard and Alison Johnson have invited us to join a group of Islanders for a special party on their farm at Ashey, inland from Ryde. Christopher Bland, a wise entrepreneur, is amongst the guests and Nick and I confidentially discuss our ideas about the Bembridge hotel. He is most enthusiastic and while we stand in the Johnsons' garden, shrouded in a strange twilight and looking ridiculous in our special cardboard dark glasses, we look down over St Helen's marsh towards Bembridge harbour in the distance and again consider the new venture. We have managed to extend the offer deadline into August.

We put the idea of the new hotel to all the staff at the Friday management meeting and they consider the option. Charlie, in particular, seems fired with enthusiasm, but Leon, who we thought would be particularly interested, especially because his grandfather once owned the hotel, is worried about staffing. We also talk to Ben and our daughters to see how they feel about us expanding the business. Naturally the extra burden would affect our family life and while we have never encouraged our off-spring to feel they will naturally take over the Seaview, the second business could be a way for one of them to enter the trade. Ben feels it is all rather too soon for him as he struggles with the complexity of the French accountancy system in Bordeaux.

Myrtle continues to cause problems. We discover it is riddled with deathwatch beetle which has to be completely eliminated. This is a cost we have not anticipated, especially as there was no indication in the survey. It is not a quick or easy job: we have to gut the cottage from top to bottom. The ceilings, walls, window frames – everything has to be either ripped out or spray treated. My initial plans have all had to change, but finally we are beginning to see the way forward and the full potential for the little cottage. During the summer property prices in Seaview, as in the rest of the country, have risen dramatically. We know that the cost of the added work to renovate Myrtle will not be wasted. Now that we can begin to see exactly how the rooms look, the fun begins. I have another scout through the interior-design magazines and books. I have a clear vision of what the final décor will be. Simple pale colours with whitewashed wooden floors and venetian blinds. A very different look to the bright colours that have been fashionable until recently. We will still have the odd splashes of colour, dark mauve, turquoise or burnt orange, in the fabrics and paintings. I want lots of different textures, the floors, walls, materials.

The ground floor is now open-plan – there are no walls left. The floors will be covered in rugs. Comfy sofas, one that converts into a double bed so that the cottage can take six. A really good airing cupboard to dry wet sailing clothes. Lots of gadgets in the kitchen: a microwave oven, toaster, kettle and fridge freezer. A small simple white bathroom with a large pressed steel bath and shower – we must get a decent pump so we can have a high-pressure shower.

Then upstairs, good comfortable beds, plenty of power points but no tellies in the rooms, and maybe a phone, well at least a phone jack socket. Duvets, not the blankets we have in the hotel. All the linen and bedspreads need to be easy to wash. Everything in the cottage will be designed to make life easy for the families that come to stay and Fay and the housekeeping staff who will have to take care of them. Most of all we want it to look striking and attractive. But in such a busy month it is hard to concentrate on anything but the hotel and the forthcoming village regatta.

As we prepare for Regatta Week, Nick and I carefully check Leon's staff rotas. The workload is high this week as the hotel needs well-drilled teams operating every day, especially on Thursday as at certain times the bars can get swamped. In past years we have had a problem with one or two members of staff going off at lunchtime and joining in the revelry only to return drunk or high and incapable of working the evening shift. It is hard for the young staff, who see everyone else having a good time and naturally want to join in. Alcohol and drug abuse is common in catering. In such a high-stress industry, anything mood-altering that helps anaesthetise tired bodies and minds is seductively welcome. But taken in excess, it just isn't good for the staff or the customers, so we nanny the young team, ensuring they fully understand their responsibilities not only to hotel guests but also to work colleagues and their own future. At the same time we continue to try to ensure they don't work excessive hours and are not put under too much stress.

Unfortunately this does not apply to Nick and myself, as we get very tired and stressed in August. In our early years, when I was doing all the cooking, I found myself, like my father before me, needing to drink just to cope with the workload and later at night to calm down and relax after a shift. I began to become dependent on the booze to help me through the busy day and eventually had to stop altogether in order to avoid my own self-destruction. Now, in spite of my collection of fine claret and vintage port in the bank vault at home, I simply don't drink. That way I don't get drunk, especially on duty. It was not easy at first but now it helps me maintain balance in my life even at these frantically busy times. It also enables me to guide and support the younger members of staff who find themselves getting into trouble with drink.

Regatta Week starts with the village dance held at the yacht club. Young and old, smart yachties and village shopkeepers, dance away to 'The Crocodile Rock' and this year's regatta spirit begins. Nick and I take turns to help as bouncers on the door. In particular we are on duty when the bars turn out at closing time at the Seaview Hotel. The punters come down the hill to the club and want to get in either for free or at a reduced price. As the dance is the main fundraiser for the regatta, enabling the village to have a magnificent firework display at the end of all the activities, we stand firm and only allow in those who have paid. It's an odd way for us to spend our Sunday night off but it's all part of village life.

Monday and Tuesday are taken up with the regatta races. One in particular, called the Carr Cup, is known as the 'Carr crash' as hundreds of assorted dinghies of all shapes and sizes clamber and bump round the first mark. This year the weather is very unpredictable and the regatta president, Peter Hunter, worries as he sees the first half of the fleet, mainly fast catamarans and lasers, all capsize as they are flattened by a rough squall out at sea. Nick who is following in his old Seaview dinghy, is about to turn back from the rolling high seas, along with a number of other sensible competitors, when he spots Paul Methuen stoically battling on out to the next mark. He realises that if Paul can keep going at over seventy, he himself can hardly turn away from the elements. Luckily all the helmsmen return safely, if drenched.

The third day of the regatta involves everyone, large and small, in the shore and swimming sports followed by a tug-of-war competition in the evening. The Seaview Hotel team, a past winner on numerous occasions, always puts on a pantomime show for the children based on the name of the current president. This year the theme is hunting, for Peter Hunter, and Will Caws arrives in his beaten-up old Landrover, firing a gun and dressed as a White Hunter, complete with Nick's grand-father's old pith helmet. Poor Nick is baking hot, running around dressed up in a lion outfit ready to be shot by the hunter before rushing back to the hotel for a quick change and a full evening's work. By the time he finishes the evening shift he is completely exhausted. Tomorrow is the busiest day of the year.

As the dawn comes up, the weather looks rough. Everything at Seaview at this time of year depends on the weather. We have had some lovely hot days recently, but there has also been a great deal of rain. When it is wet, no one can sit outside. So everyone has to squeeze into the two bars and along the narrow corridor. It's uncomfortable and bad for business. It means we can only serve half the number and that no one will be really happy except in the restaurant. If the weather looks bad on regatta day then Islanders don't bother to come over to join in the celebrations. Those who do line the corridors and end up spilling drink and cigarette ash over the hotel carpet and walls. Ace Cleaners have to be called in again. It's bad for the interior décor and it's bad for the bar take.

The forecast is not good. Nick and I get up early to prepare for the regatta breakfast. The builders Caws & Hermans play a major role in the running of the regatta as well as supplying the hotel tug-of-war team. Each year they erect the president's staging for his speech and prize-giving. They prepare the course for the shore sports, swimming and greasy pole. Then on Thursday they haul all the boats in and out of the water.

The beautiful old rowing skiffs are carefully maintained and stored by Michael Warren. A week before the regatta they emerge from Michael's store and are filled with water to check they are still seaworthy. Then they appear resplendent on Quay Rocks, going in and out all day for race after race. Sometimes, for the singles, they only have one person on board, while other races like the Randan need three oarsmen plus a cox as the team plough down the long course in front of the hotel. Then at the end of the day, almost by magic, they disappear into the boat store for another year.

For a treat, on regatta morning, Will Caws and Rob Hermans invite their workmen, plus the president of the regatta and one or two other helpers, for a special breakfast at the hotel. Over the years the breakfast guest-list has grown, as past presidents continue to attend, and now the party is well over thirty. Today everyone from the village policeman to Paul Methuen makes their way into the Sunshine Restaurant for the special party. Sir Norman Fowler and Clare Francis share a table with Barry Allen the carpenter and Mick Shiner the bricklayer. Nick and I are geared up ready to ensure that, as for any major function at the Seaview, everyone is served at the same time and has everything they need. Meanwhile we need to keep a careful eye on our hotel guests, who require their own breakfast at exactly the same time. It is a busy start to a busy day, but with an extra chef on duty and twice the waiting staff, things pass off smoothly.

Once breakfast is over Nick and I ensure everything is in place in the hotel before preparing to take part in the forty-and-over mixed doubles. Paul Methuen, our regular cox each year, appears in his yachting whites and Royal Yacht Squadron cap. The long course out at sea is not easy, especially when the wind is blowing, and all my enthusiasm drains as I look out at the rough water. I know this is one event we have no chance of winning but in truly British style we at least take part. Paul, hardly the lightest cox, is great company and fills us with confidence. Richard Bowtell, who organises all the rowing events, announces over the tannoy system that heavier coxes are an advantage in the rougher conditions as they help keep the bow up out of the waves. Paul is delighted his extra pounds are an advantage and off we go. 'In, out, in, out,' Paul calls as he steers the skiff, while Nick and I try to synchronise our oars, and dig into the loppy water. Exhausted, we cross the finish line and slowly row back to the shore knowing we have won no trophies today.

The bars are open all day and have a steady stream of customers. By the evening the whole hotel is crowded but as the weather is unsettled we are not swamped. At nine thirty-five the first firework goes up with a huge bang. The front is packed with masses of people gazing into the sky, going oohh . . . ahhh . . . This year we definitely have the best display ever and after what seems like an age (and a fortune), the excited crowds return to the bars for a serious evening's drinking. Because of the volume of people wandering up and down to the shore we use plastic glasses. The night ends well after midnight, with our exhausted staff clearing up the mess, but at least they don't have piles of washing up glasses before preparing for another early breakfast.

During this frantic week our dogs Cleo and Millie go away on holiday. Cleo doesn't like the bang of the starter guns at the yacht club, she likes the cannons for the rowing regatta even less, and she simply hates the fireworks. So both dogs go on holiday to stay with Anthony and Alex Goddard up at Goddard's brewery at the back of Seaview. Millie was born at the Goddards' and loves rabbiting with her mother and sister, and Cleo is most grateful to be free to chase across green fields rather than quake and shiver in fear of the terrible noises in Seaview. Part of me, exhausted after all the regatta activity, envies their countryside retreat.

Friday is the President's Party and Dinghy Dance night. The President of the regatta gives a party for anything up to three hundred people, all of whom help in one way or another over Seaview Regatta Week. When Nick was president it was a nightmare trying to organise how we would hold such a huge party in our house, while still trying to run the hotel.

Every year before the Dinghy Dance large parties book tables in the restaurant and others arrive early to bag tables outside or in the bars. They all want to eat before moving on down to the club for an evening's dancing. This year our children have invited over forty friends for a pre-dance party in our house. Pip received her A-level results yesterday and though she is disappointed with her Maths result, she has done really well in Biology and got an A in Geography. She and Ben prepare dustbin-loads of Pimms and our front garden is swarming with more guests than outside the hotel. The evening runs smoothly both at the party and in the bars and restaurants. That night, after finishing service and clearing up, Nick and I wander down to listen outside to the band playing at the yacht club dance. We return along the seafront to our usual spot and quietly sit and gaze out to sea. It is a clear night but there is a definite nip in the air, we have nearly finished another season. We turn up the high street and reconsider the Bembridge hotel.

As the August Bank Holiday approaches all the staff are now very tired. We begin to organise the end-of-season party. Before the summer staff leave we give everyone a special dinner at the Old Fort Restaurant. One or two students who have been training with us for a number of years will also be moving on in September, and we are sad to see our hard-working staff go, but, rather like young adolescents in a family, it is important for their development for them to move on and gain experience elsewhere.

It's a problem that everyone is so tired. We need to recruit replacements quickly so the permanent staff aren't left with extra duties to cover. Barbara and I work on an advertisement to go in the local paper and organise who will conduct the interviews. Josh in particular is very helpful and details of his interview experience will be good for him to take back to the Blue Mountain school in Australia. At the same time, I compose the invitation to the staff party on the first Sunday in September. Morale in any business is extremely important. Part of good leadership requires a constant understanding and appreciation of the mood of all employees. Parties and informal gatherings help to bond the team and boost morale, as well as showing appreciation for hard work. Everyone loves to see Nick, normally so formal and traditional, perform karaoke.

Bad weather after the regatta results in many families leaving the village immediately after the weekend. Suddenly there is space to park cars and tables free in both the restaurants and bars. Then, just as we begin to think it is all over, the sun returns. The forecast for the bank holiday is excellent and the village is again full, with holiday festivities for the weekend. Once again on Saturday night the bars and restaurants are full to capacity. By now the team in the kitchen are so geared up that they sail through the evening without a hitch. Everyone, staff and guests alike, has tanned faces and an end-of-season glow.

After a hectic bank holiday Sunday lunch, we speed through the busy evening and by Monday morning cars are packed up for the journey home. There is one more crab ramekin and bubble and squeak before the families set off back to the mainland, their businesses and a new school term. We begin to count the weekend takings and are able to have a look back over the figures for August. Things have been good, but not outstanding, the poor weather especially during and after the regatta has taken its toll. But all in all, the summer has been a success and there is very little room to improve our takings as we are already at capacity this month.

Nick and I say goodbye to the last of the bank holiday guests and decide not to buy the Bembridge hotel. We know it is a good business at an attractive price and would not hesitate to encourage a younger couple to go for it. But we have done that particular voyage. We cherish what we have created at the Seaview and the way it works for all of us. Sometimes astute business decisions are based on knowing your own limitations. It would be so easy to arrogantly forge ahead and it might well bring big financial rewards. But for Nick and me the bottom line is not just about money and profit, it is about our whole working philosophy. We decide at this stage in our life not to jeopardise what we have created and nurtured by adding to our stress with the burden of another business. What we really want is to continue to enjoy our time at the Seaview. I know that professional manuals may say that if the business isn't growing and moving forward it is going backwards. But I don't think life is always about business manuals.

The latest edition of the *Which? Hotel Guide* arrives and the Seaview is described as the 'Small hotel with a huge personality'. What more could we want?